Reeva

Reeva

A Mother's Story

June Steenkamp
with Sarah Edworthy

sphere

SPHERE

First published in Great Britain in 2014 by Sphere

Copyright © June Steenkamp 2014

Edited by Sarah Edworthy

The moral right of the author has been asserted.

A CIP catalogue record for this book
is available from the British Library.

Hardback ISBN 978-0-7515-5871-5
C format ISBN 978-0-7515-5872-2

Typeset in Bembo by M Rules
Printed and bound in Great Britain by
Clays Ltd, St Ives plc

Papers used by Sphere are from well-managed forests
and other responsible sources.

MIX
Paper from
responsible sources
FSC
www.fsc.org
FSC® C104740

Sphere
An imprint of
Little, Brown Book Group
100 Victoria Embankment
London EC4Y 0DY

An Hachette UK Company
www.hachette.co.uk

www.littlebrown.co.uk

To my angel Reeva

Letter to Reeva, on your eighteenth birthday

19.8.2001

My dearest, darling daughter,

I wish you up to the moon and around the world in wonders or whatever comes to mind that you wish for.

I want to tell you now that you are a full-grown beautiful woman how proud I am of you. You were a gift from God and I have treasured every moment we have shared to date. Now is the time for you to spread your wings and fly in your own direction. I have no worries about this because you are sensible, intelligent and very clued up.

It's only your heart that may get you in trouble because it's on your sleeve.

I want to tell you how proud I am of you. You always care for others and you are not self-absorbed. You are dedicated in your future and I see not only the exterior, although it's beautiful, but inside I see a wealth of qualities reside there.

I love you so much and I just want the best of everything for you.

Happy 18th Birthday Reeva,

Love,

Mom xxx

Letter to June on her fifty-sixth birthday from Reeva
26 September 2003
A whole year has gone by again, reminding us that time waits for no one and that every passing moment is an opportunity to make life that much more sweeter.

I'm happy that I can spend each day with you and grab new opportunities, each time they pass, with you at my side.

I wouldn't choose anybody else to take this journey with, and nobody else can take your place.

Today is a day to say thanks for being a great person, a beautiful woman, a trusted friend, a devoted mother and most of all – the best you that you can be!

I love you very much.

Enjoy the flowers, pressie, cake and loads of kisses and love – all for you on this day – and tomorrow and the next day and the next . . .

Your compadre forever
Reeves xxxxx
PS: Dad says ditto for all of the above ☺

14 February 2013

Dromedaris Road, Seaview, Port Elizabeth

The beginning of the nightmare.

We are up and about before dawn as usual. Barry sets off for the short drive to the stables at Arlington Racecourse to prepare his horses for their morning exercise. I potter out to greet the overzealous dogs – Boyki and Gypsy the boerboels, Dax and Madonna the Jack Russells and little Moby Dick, Reeva's dachshund – fighting through playful paws and swishing tails to give them their breakfast. The sun rises just before 6 a.m., promising another balmy summer day. I make tea and start getting myself ready to go to work. At my age I joke my face needs three applications of sand and three of cement. I'm preoccupied with thoughts about the day ahead, about supervising progress at the Barking Spider, a pub we're building at the Greenbushes Hotel on the Old Cape Road, when my mobile phone rings.

Really? At this time of the morning?

A voice introduces himself as Detective Hilton Botha.

'Hello, is that June Steenkamp?'

'Yes.'

'Do you have a daughter, Reeva?'

'Yes.'

'There has been a terrible accident.'

'What kind of accident?'

'Your daughter has been shot.'

Pause.

'You'd better tell me RIGHT NOW if she's dead or alive.'

'I'm sorry. I'm afraid she has passed on.'

The detective is polite, concerned, saying he wants to inform me before I get in the car and hear it on the radio news. He says he thinks it looks like an 'open-and-shut' case. *'There were only two people present – your daughter and Oscar with the gun.'*

I've heard enough.

I'm hysterical, screaming, sobbing uncontrollably. This cannot be true. The worst thing in the world has happened – it really has – this beautiful, perfect child of mine is dead. We are, we were, mother and daughter with such a strong connection. We are the best of friends, so close we talk about everything. We even have a pact that, if one of us dies, we will let the other know with a sign that we are okay and in a good place.

How can Reeva be dead? I can still hear her chattering away to me last night, telling me that she is arriving at her boyfriend's house to cook him a romantic Valentine's Day dinner, that they are planning a quiet evening, that she's sending money for our cable TV subscription so that we can watch her in the new series of *Tropika Island of Treasure*, which airs this weekend, and that she loves me. Big kiss!

I visualise the police searching for my number on the contacts list on Reeva's phone – *Mommy BlackBerry* – while she ... I don't let my mind go further. Imagine answering your phone at seven o'clock in the morning and hearing that your daughter is dead from gunshot wounds. It's just not real. It's devastating. Our lodger David hears my anguish and comes to try and help. He says he'll call my good friends Claire and Sam, and they are here in minutes, not knowing what to do because now I'm almost mute with shock. I manage to phone Barry and tell him he must come home immediately.

Barry drives home from the stables thinking one of the older dogs has died. He misunderstood my hysterical sobs, because I would be upset about the dogs. When he arrives and hears the bitter truth, he goes into a truly terrifying state of shock, trembling violently, and asking over and over again how, *how*, can Reeva, our beautiful baby, be dead. She was our whole life, our *laat lammetjie*, a precious late lamb, the only child we had together, the backbone of our extended family and the glue – let's be frank – in our relationship. In the few minutes it took the detective to communicate the news, our lives seem to have crumbled like a sandcastle knocked by a freak wave on the beach.

The detective's words echo in my head: *There were only two people present – your daughter and Oscar with the gun.* What terrible, terrible thing could have happened between two young people to precipitate this? They had known each other for scarcely three months. Reeva, I knew, was excited about and wary of this new relationship in equal measure. When it started, his infatuation was too much, but after a break, she told me she had decided to give her all to the relationship despite nagging doubts about their compatibility. He was hard to please. He could be moody and volatile. But she loved him, and admired him, especially for all he had overcome in life, and how he used that as a power to inspire other people. That was her dream too. She was a caring girl, a nurturer by nature. She wanted to help others. Was it as I had feared when she was eighteen: that her heart had got her into trouble? Did she suffer because her expectations of love were not met?

8

Barry's in such a state, and more friends are turning up at the house with condolences. But what can they say? They are shocked. It's too much for all of us. People from the stables start arriving to support us, the jockeys and members of the racing community whom Barry has known for the last fifty years. Somehow I manage to phone Barry's younger brother Michael, who is very involved in the church, a lay minister giving occasional sermons and so on. He runs a Christian drug rehabilitation centre outside Cape Town. He's a lovely kind man and the only one who can calm Barry down. Barry, nearly seventy, is diabetic and not in the best of health. He's a big, gentle man, but when he gets stressed – and right now he's in torment, trying to absorb the fact that some guy he doesn't know has murdered his beloved daughter – he goes from 0 to 300 in five seconds. We need to keep him calm for his health.

I experience all this in a dreamlike, practically comatose state.

Almost immediately the press are outside our little rented house in Seaview; reporters, cars, vans, cameras, cables and mushrooming satellite dishes, all set to camp outside for weeks. Flowers and notes of sympathy start arriving from all over the world. The news of our daughter's violent death swamps national and international media, with one TV reporter saying it is arguably as big a story as the release of

Nelson Mandela in 1990. Princess Charlene of Monaco sends a bouquet. It seems surreal to think that something so cataclysmic has happened to connect a royal palace in Europe with our modest suburban street in South Africa and touched someone living in a world so different from our own that they're moved to send us flowers and heartfelt condolences. Soon the house is bursting with flowers, their scent overwhelming. Our home, which already had hundreds of photos of Reeva, resembles a shrine. People come to the gate to try and talk to us. They leave messages and food and more flowers.

At the heart of lurid speculation gripping the world's news sites, the established facts on the Breaking News feed are few: Reeva was shot in a toilet cubicle in the bathroom of the Paralympian athlete's R4.5 million luxury villa in one of South Africa's most prestigious gated communities in the early hours of 14 February. Four shots were fired through the locked toilet door. Reeva was hit three times and died of her wounds. A 9mm pistol was seized by police at the scene. The man who shot her through a locked door told his family that he thought an intruder was in his bathroom and that he shot through the door out of fear. This turns out to be the start of a process that lasts through to the end of the trial, where Barry and I pore over every snippet of information, every piece of 'evidence' we learn about from the media, to figure out what happened in the hours and minutes leading up to her death. We want to find some comfort from being able to think our daughter died without suffering, without any notion of what was about to happen to her, but everything points us in the opposite direction. We look at everything through the prism of knowing Reeva so well, and imagining all too clearly what she must have gone through.

Barry looks to see if there is any personal message from the man who shot her among the tributes, but there is only a bouquet sent with an impersonal line from his management agency office.

How I get through the rest of the day and night I don't know. We are lucky to have such amazing friends and family. When I slip into some sort of slumber on that first night after her death, Reeva appears to me in a dream in a long white dress. She looks so beautiful. 'Mama,' she says. 'I hope he doesn't shoot me again.' Now in my dreams she only appears as a little girl, and I feed her and nurture her. That first night is the only time she comes to me as her radiant grown-up self.

When I see a picture in the Friday newspaper of the man who has shot her so grievously, I realise I don't even know him. Yet he is so familiar to the world at large. Newsreaders and reporters express incredulity: how can a sporting hero of his stature, celebrated for his charity work, become a murder suspect? How can a 'celebrity romance' end in such a way? It's hard to match up the story with our understanding of our daughter's life. To the outside world, the shock is that *he* can be implicated in this violent crime; to us, the shock is that our beloved daughter's life has been extinguished.

I've never heard of the Blade Runner. We are country people and we didn't sit glued to the TV for the 2012 London Games where I learn he made history by becoming the first amputee sprinter to compete at the Olympics: our TV screen is permanently tuned into Tellytrack, the channel dedicated to horse racing, the sport which has always been Barry's life. I had never heard of him before Reeva started talking about him on the phone – and that was scarcely three months ago. She still hadn't spoken of him to her father, which meant that she was unsure about the relationship. With Barry, she'd keep quiet about a relationship until she felt confident that it was stable. But this man whose face I'm looking at for the first time in the newspaper, this stranger, has hurt our child, shot her, not once but shot her repeatedly until she was dead, shot her in the hip and the head above her right ear and in the elbow, shot her with Black Talon bullets that 'open up' when they enter the body, destroying flesh, bones and internal organs.

This is the unbearable thing: thinking of Reeva behind that locked toilet door, waiting for God to save her. She was a strong, strong Christian and she would have been waiting behind that door, petrified, believing God would save her. Only later would I realise that God had to take her because the injuries to her head were so bad. One bullet blew the brains out of her skull. If she had survived, she would have been in a coma, and she could not live without her brilliant mind, her vibrant faculties.

This image is the thing Barry and I agonise over. In our worst imaginings, we picture how scared she must have been to retreat behind that door, and lock it, with no one to protect her. As parents who've always doted on our child, there's no escape from a wretched feeling of helplessness as we relive our daughter's last minutes on Earth, envisioning her cowering from a shower of bullets fired by the man she loved. As her warm-hearted Xhosa language teacher Mrs Ntlangu says to me, 'No one deserves to die by a gun, but I really hate it when someone shoots and carries on shooting a person to death, an unarmed helpless person.'

The pain only gets worse. I don't know how I will get through these next few days, surfacing every morning knowing I will never hear my daughter's voice again, never see her smiling elfin face, never watch her throw back her head and laugh throatily, never send my little love fairies via SMS to make her feel better when she's ill, never again hold her when she cries. How can I accept she has just gone? Gone for ever.

Nothing anyone can say will help. Friends bring their children to be with me and comfort me. Claire, my friend of thirty years, comes over with her daughter Shelly. Tara Laing, a racehorse trainer, brings her son Ewan and he brings his little blanky, his soother, which he gives to me. The children sleep next to me for comfort. People don't know how to commiserate with words in such a desperate situation, but the children's cosy physical presence gives me some solace.

My brother-in-law, Michael, helps us to think about the funeral. In fact he and his wife Lyn and daughters Kim and Sharon organise it for us. They're wonderful people. Michael is under immense stress, acting as spokesman for the family. The enormity of the media frenzy is something our normal, low-key family has never experienced. We feel surrounded by chaos and it is impossible to start grieving. Michael and Kim go through the steps of organising the funeral arrangements, ticking boxes on the list of options, almost on autopilot. Do we want roses? Yes. Do we want this kind of casket? Yes.

After an autopsy her body is flown home from Johannesburg to Dove's Funeral Services in Port Elizabeth and we, all her family, wait one by one to see her and say our private goodbyes. Eventually it is my turn and I walk slowly into the room for what I know is the worst moment of my life. I can only see her pale face. Her body is swaddled in sheets and a white silk scarf is swathed around her head to cover her injuries. I am told not to move anything. She is waxy and lifeless, but she still looks beautiful, she is still my Reeva. I kiss her and whisper, 'I love you so much, darling, and I'm going to miss you. We will meet again.' Oh, how I wish that meeting is soon – and then my legs give way and I fall to the floor. People pick me up and carry me outside.

I insist they take me back in to her. It is too hard to walk away for the last time.

The funeral ceremony is held at 11 a.m. on 19 February at Victoria Park Crematorium Chapel, in Walmer, just five days after she met her death. Port Elizabeth is known as the Windy City, but the day of the funeral is unnaturally still and calm. Often, if someone has been killed, and the circumstances lead to a criminal trial, the body is not released for some time. An investigation normally delays a funeral. I remember people remarking how quickly we were allowed to reclaim her. I'm not compos mentis – I think by now I've been prescribed sedative medication to help me cope with my grief – so I don't try to understand why it is happening so swiftly.

How I sit through the funeral of my own daughter, I don't know. I don't remember much. I'm travelling through mist and fog. I'm not really here. I remember little snapshots. The memorial hall of the crematorium chapel jam-packed with people. Reeva's pale wooden casket covered in St Joseph's lilies, a symbol of purity. There's a long red carpet down the central aisle. Friends embrace me and whisper words of comfort. We have Psalm 23, the Lord Is My Shepherd. People are invited to stand and share their memories ... Strangers from her life in the bright lights of Johannesburg take their five minutes to claim Reeva as their 'best friend'; who are they all? Others, who I know well, also feel emboldened to speak. I recall my grandson Nicholas saying such beautiful things about her and how much he loved her as they grew up together, as close in age as siblings. It is hard for him to get through his speech, but I am proud of him ... I remember the bereft look on the face of my niece Kim's teenage daughter, Gypsy, who also stands up boldly and tells how she was going down the wrong path but Reeva encouraged her not to waste her life and helped her turn herself around. Other young people to whom she made a difference express their devastation over losing her. It is all a painful blur. Reeva had a magic heart of gold and she was close to so many of them.

A minibus full of nuns and teachers from St Dominic's Priory School draws up outside and her former classmates line up in an arc formation around the chapel door to embrace her in death as she had them in life. That is such a beautiful tribute. Many of them wear their old school uniform, those well-worn navy-and-gold striped blazers, and these are friends who are nearly thirty! 'Everything about her – the reception she gave everyone – was amazing. She was so vibrant,' one of her former classmates says to me. 'I remember she tried to be a part of us. She made the time to learn my language, Xhosa, which meant the world.' Another young man tells me, 'She was all love, warmth, hugs and smiles, that is how we remember her.' It is very touching.

So many people come to pay their respects to Reeva. People she has reached out to in all walks of life come two hours early to make sure of a seat in the church; friends from her years growing up in Port Elizabeth, like Wayne her first love; friends from Johannesburg where she moved to pursue a career in modelling when she was twenty-two. Friends like Kristin, who studied law with Reeva in PE and also moved to Johannesburg; she comes half an hour early and finds the chapel full. Fellow mourners squeeze up on the pew to let her sit. Poor Kristin. Her former high school is right next to the crematorium and she often used to see the puffs of black smoke rising up from the chimney, never imagining she'd so soon be inside, saying farewell to a close friend in the prime of life. Francois Hougaard, the South African rugby union player and briefly a boyfriend of Reeva's with whom she remained good friends, arrives nattily dressed in a suit and dark glasses to pay his respects. Her lovely longtime ex-boyfriend

Warren Lahoud – the man we thought she'd marry – comes with his mother Cecilia. Gina Myers, a make-up artist, attends with her parents Cecil and Desi and sister Kim, the family with whom Reeva lodged for the last seven months. TV presenter Pearl Thusi and the DJs, musicians and models who starred alongside Reeva on the *Tropika Island of Treasure* reality programme, arrive as a group. Nelson Mandela Bay deputy mayor Nancy Sihlwayi attends the service on behalf of South African women after attending a protest against gender violence outside the Port Elizabeth High Court. Former Eastern Cape premier Nosimo Balindlela expresses her sadness with moving words: 'This child is the daughter of Africa. She was humble and even from listening to her friends speak of her, she was just such a loving and caring girl. I am deeply saddened by this incident.'

Quite a number sit in their cars outside. Some because they can't fit into the building; some sit privately because it is too much for them to witness the finality of Reeva's cremation. One friend, whose wife Reeva had sat with for many days when she was dying of cancer – talking to her, painting her nails, spending time with her – pays vigil in his car outside. He is overwhelmed.

The Order of Service is printed with a portrait of Reeva – so young, so beautiful, only twenty-nine – next to the poignant poem, *God's Gift, A Child:*

'I'll lend you for a little while a child of mine,' He said.
'For you to love the while she lives.
It may be six or seven years or twenty-nine or three
But will you till I call her back take care of her for Me?

She'll bring her charms to gladden you
And should her stay be brief —
You'll have her lovely memories as solace for your grief.
I cannot promise you she'll stay
Since all on Earth return
But there are lessons taught down there
I want this child to learn.

I've looked the whole world over
And in my search for teachers true
And from the throngs that crowd life's lane
I have selected you!
Now will you give her all your love
Nor think the labour vain
Nor hate me when I come to call, to take her back again?

I fancied that I heard them say, 'Dear Lord Thy Will Be Done
For all the joy the child shall bring, the risk of grief we'll run.
We'll shelter her with tenderness — we'll love her while we may
And for all the happiness we've known, forever grateful stay!

Reeva

And should the Angels call her, much sooner than we planned,
We'll brave the bitter grief that comes,
And try to understand.'

The funeral takes place at the same time as Oscar Pistorius – there, I've said his name – appears in court in Pretoria charged with her murder.

The irony is that on any other occasion this gathering of some of South Africa's most gifted and admired young people would be a celebration of something. Reeva would have loved the gathering together of so many of her dearest family and friends, but she is not here to see it. Her absence is why we have all come together. The reality of her death is hard to come to terms with. We're doing what the poem urges, braving the bitter grief and trying to understand. For us, it is a debilitating family tragedy, a shocking personal loss which we have to start trying to come to terms with under the spotlight of a global audience fascinated by a looming criminal trial that will seek to determine the truth of what really happened to our daughter. The impartial words of the news bulletins that keep replaying on radio and television sound clinical and alien, impossible to relate to the fate of our bubbly, cheeky, vivacious, loving Reeva:

14 February 2013

We can confirm a twenty-nine-year-old woman died on the scene from gunshot wounds. A twenty-six-year-old man has been arrested and charged with murder ...

Friends of the slain model express their shock ...

Coming up: a report on the gruesome end of a tragic love match ...

Reeva is famous now. All over the world people express their love for her and their outrage that such a crime could be committed against an innocent, loving young woman. She is alive in the global consciousness as a vibrant personality whom people want to embrace and hold on to as a symbol of all too common a form of injustice. Her image flits across the TV screen and smiles down from shelves of magazines. But she, the Reeva who was simply our beloved child, is dead. She's gone and never coming back. It is hard to absorb our very personal loss and the irony of the context in which her death is being discussed and debated.

There is a constant feeling of surveillance as the press continue to follow the story of how a beautiful model in the prime of her life and career could meet such a violent end at the hands of a national hero. To be honest, I hardly notice the presence of the cameras. I am just trying to get through each day, but every so often I have to endure the low antics of some member of the press and that makes our life so much more difficult. We have enough to deal with, trying to bear our loss, and then you have these other things: reporters sneaking through your front gate and into your home to join the grieving families that are here, and going so far as to pretend that they knew Reeva and they were her friend. We hear of social network sites set up by fans of the man who killed her to 'take his side': Team Oscar. There are rumours that he has reached out and made contact with us. Whose business is that but ours? It is true his representatives proposed a meeting, but it is too early. I don't want to speak to him. What could I possibly say to him? I don't even want to look at him, you know? He's taken the most precious thing that we had away from us.

Our landlady came to the funeral and then 'heard' via a news agency that we had no money and we wouldn't be able to pay our rent. Soon after the funeral we receive a letter from her giving us two months' notice to leave. Don't worry, we'll be out in one month, I tell her. Who wants to stay where you're not welcome? We start packing up all our belongings and move to a small house out in the Greenbushes, next to our dear friend Claire – so it was meant to be, probably, and we appreciate the peace and quiet here now. Some media follow us here too. Barry often goes out of the house to smoke and then the press will print a story asking how Barry can afford to smoke if we don't have any money. It's a terrible intrusion.

Horror, disbelief, grief come in waves. I find it difficult to eat properly. I feel no appetite. Weight starts to fall off me. Eating is about sustaining yourself, and you don't have the will to look after yourself when your most precious loved one is dead. Days, weeks, months mean nothing to me now. I am not engaged in the real world. For a long time I can't go out, go anywhere. How can I when my daughter's face is every-where – on TV, newspapers, magazines. To think how I used to rush out to buy magazines and publications whenever Reeva told me she was appearing in one. And now I'm avoiding them. There is no escaping the brutal truth. I am too much of a wreck. I can't believe she's just disappeared from our lives. She gave us lots of love, lots of attention. She was a wonderful daughter. If I think now that I'd like to phone her, I can't. I can't contact her. I can't see her. As mother and daughter we were so close a unit even after she'd moved to Johannesburg that whenever I'd bump into friends in the shopping mall or somewhere, they'd never say 'Hello, June', they'd just say 'How's Reeva?' Our bond was so strong that long after she moved away to pursue her modelling career, she still needed me. I lived for her. I was so proud of her. We talked about anything and everything. I miss her ter-ribly, every moment of every day.

I find an old letter Reeva wrote to me when she was seventeen. She used to come and help me at the spaza shop, an informal convenience store I ran for fifteen years up at the racecourse where Barry had his horses. On this occasion a friend 'needed' her and she felt bad about leaving me to work alone in the shop. *Remember the day I went to* Cinderella *– I cried and I cried because you weren't there and you were all I ever depended on + it's scary, even now, as an adult, to walk alone,* she wrote back in May 2001. *OK, maybe I'm a "mommy's girl" like dad always says, but SO WHAT!!! – I like it + I like you . . . love you. There's nothing wrong with that, right? Neh, I don't think so! I just know, deep down inside, that without you, I would be nothing + no one – NO ONE – would be there to pick up the pieces . . . I love you with all my life and my entire being . . . Reeves.*

Ever since the events of 14 February 2013, I wake up every night at 3 a.m. with my head full of her and vivid snatches of dreams about her. Barry and I both wake up crying. It's hard, you know. As soon as you stir from sleep, your brain goes in that direction. It's set in my body clock now. Three o'clock, I wake up. I wonder, is that because that's the time it happened? I hear Barry sitting outside on the porch. I know he's smoking and that tears are streaming down his cheeks. We speak in the depths of night – because we both get down from it, experiencing different moods at different times, and that's not easy on a relationship either – and I ask Barry, What is the worst part for you? He says he keeps going over those minutes she was locked behind the toilet door. He imagines her begging for her life. He agonises over what was going through her mind: Where is anyone? Who is going to save me? She never in her life would be thinking he's going to kill her. She wouldn't be thinking of guns and violence aimed at her by her own boyfriend, the man she called her Boo.

That's our nightmare. Both of us are haunted by the same nightmare. The vision of Reeva suffering this terrible trauma. Her terror and helplessness. Her yells for help piercing the silent night air. From the day she was born we protected her, but from this we couldn't protect her. Why couldn't I have warned her that this person could be capable of such hideous violence? Because he shot her not just once, but bang, bang, bang, bang with 9mm bullets, until she was dead. How could she, who was so alert to the ill treatment of innocent women, end up with a person who could aim a gun towards another human being and shoot her dead?

Oscar's story I don't believe. It seems to me he did not look for her when he says he thought he heard intruders. Not one of his actions suggests he felt protective towards her. A lot of people have guns in South Africa and everyone knows, bottom line, you never ever shoot if you have not checked where your own people are: never, ever, ever. I work out in my own mind what I think happened. They had a fight, a horrible argument, and she fled to the bathroom with her mobile and locked the door. It was 3 a.m. She was dressed in shorts and a top. Her clothes were packed, ready to leave. I think he may have shot once and then he had to go on and kill her because she would have been able to tell the world what really happened, what he's really like. Why did he point a gun at a locked door? Why did he have so many guns in the first place? It's a simple fact, if he didn't have a gun, she'd be alive today. You know how many of the neighbours heard the screams – blood-curdling screams, one lady said, *blood-curdling screams for help*, and her window was open, her balcony door was open, and she was a neighbour living close by.

Now it's a matter of trying to live without her. We both try and immerse ourselves in things we know she loved and things we know she would love to see us doing. She was in the middle of reading *The Book Thief* by Markus Zusak when she died and we both read that to feel close to her. I have all her books in my bedroom. I have her white linen on the bed. It's a comfort to know she once slept in it and that somehow her essence must still be there. I wear her clothes and jewellery – the little jacket with a furry hood, the embellished denim jacket, her guinea-fowl feather earrings, the little leather cuff with a horsehead clasp – and I spray myself with her Narciso Rodriguez perfume to drink in her presence. She had quite a collection of scents: more than forty perfumes, beautiful bottles of eau de toilette and lots of aromatic candles. She loved to create a calm and serene atmosphere in her room. We have her cook books – Nigella Lawson's *How to Be a Domestic Goddess* and Mary Berry's *Great British Bake Off.* She loved making banana bread once a week to take in to her friends in the model agency. And she loved Barry's way with horses, so it's wonderful he is now back working with horses at his new place in Fairview. She used to ride often before she fell from a horse and broke her back when she was twenty. After the accident, it was still natural for her to go and help at the stables, feeding horses, mucking out, pushing the wheelbarrow. She was a country girl at heart. As a young girl, if she knew Barry was going to have a winner, she'd go to lead his horses into the ring. She shared his excitement and kept cuttings of his victories. She was very proud of him.

I find myself thinking of her all the time, hearing her warm voice, her chatter, her mock admonishments. I wish I could see her throw back her head and laugh again. Whenever I do my hair, I hear her saying, 'Don't forget the back, Mama!' because whenever I iron my hair straight I tend to miss out the back section, leaving little squiggles, and she was always so polished. I open the fridge and think how horrified she'd be by the state of it. The first thing she did whenever she visited us was go straight to the fridge and clear out all the things that had been hanging around in it for months. I usually wait until things walk out themselves. A song keeps playing on the radio and makes me cry. When I first hear the lyrics sung by Labrinth and Emeli Sandé — *Would you let me see beneath you're beautiful? Would you let me see beneath you're perfect?* — it reminds me so much of Reeva. I talk to Powder, her blue-point Siamese cat, and say 'It's Reeva' and he cries. He's fourteen now.

Barry and I gradually identify objects that we will treasure as mementos that Reeva gave us throughout her twenty-nine years. We take a second look at two paintings we'd had up for years on the kitchen wall. Reeva used to paint a lot in her early teens and when your child gives you some lovely coloured images on canvas you keep them, don't you? We never understood these paintings. Now we see that they're spooky. They seem prophetic. In the first one, she painted a man under a tree, holding his gun like a prized possession, and close to him is a beautiful dark-haired young girl in a white dress with angel wings, and a ladder going up to heaven. This is Reeva. She was naturally a wavy-haired brunette, just like the figure she painted. And the girl's hands are over her mouth. She's expressing horror, shock. She's petrified.

Can you believe it? It's almost as if she had a premonition.

The second painting comprises two canvases. The left-hand side one shows a figure crouched in fear in a small space, as Reeva may have been in the toilet cubicle when she was shot. Shortly after her death, there was an identical sketch of her in this position in the South African *Sunday Times*. The figure she painted even has marks on her legs where the bullets in real life grazed her and she has depicted one broken arm as well. How strange is that? Oscar's first bullet went into her hip, a Black Talon bullet which exploded inside her. His second bullet went through her fingers and shattered her elbow, so her arm was completely lame. And the right-hand canvas, which she mounted next to the crouching figure as if they had to be interpreted together, is painted solid, blank, blood red – oblivion.

It is weird. Twice over, I think she had a premonition. They were painted for a reason. We've had the paintings around for years because of the cheery strong colours, but these are now gory and macabre for us. We never stopped to analyse the expression on the figure's face, but now I see it's Reeva, shocked, afraid, and utterly bewildered.

On 14 April 2013, Oscar is back in the news for getting bail set at one million rand. He is required to live at an undisclosed address, hand in his two South African passports and report twice a week to a police station in Pretoria.

We see pictures of Oscar partying. He's drinking, flirting, photographed with an *FHM* model, he doesn't seem like someone who has lost the love of his life. I have forgiven him. I have to – that's my religion. It's not healthy to carry evil thoughts about him because it will only destroy me, eat me up. But I can't forget what he's done. I hate what he's done to my child, the girl I gave birth to, a child who never gave us any trouble, who worked hard at school and earned thirteen distinctions during her law studies at Nelson Mandela Metropolitan University in Port Elizabeth. She studied conscientiously for her Bachelor of Laws degree, then moved to Johannesburg and focused on her modelling as part of her strategy to become a person with a profile, so that she could return to a career in law as someone with a voice to speak out against violence against women in South Africa. Inside that beautiful girl was a heart of gold. She lit up a room. She loved people. I try hard to live up to the quotes that Reeva held dear. The last few thoughts she tweeted before her death give an indication of her loving, generous outlook:

Before you lift your pen or raise your voice to criticise, acknowledge peoples' circumstances. You don't know their strengths, their journey.

On 9 February, four days before she drove to Pretoria that last fateful time, she had tweeted:

I woke up this morning in a safe home. Not everyone did. Speak out about the rape of individuals in South Africa. RIP Annie Booysen #rape #crime #sayNO.

Reeva, like everyone in South Africa, had been deeply troubled by the barbaric rape and murder of teenager Anene Booysen ten days previously in Bredasdorp in the Western Cape. The seventeen-year-old, known as Annie, had been enjoying a happy evening out with friends. Walking home with a twenty-two-year-old man she had a crush on, she ended up being gang-raped, grotesquely disembowelled and left for dead at a construction site. It seems incomprehensible now that Reeva and Annie Booysen are twinned by fate in the public consciousness, two beautiful big-hearted young women killed by men they admired, two names jointly remembered in protests about violence against innocent women.

On 13 February, Reeva asked her 40,000 or so followers:

What do you have up your sleeve for your love tomorrow??? #getexcited #Valentine'sDay.

She loved making an occasion of Valentine's Day. In 2012 she was staying in Cape Town with her cousin Kim. As usual, she wanted to make a big fuss of the day and went to a lot of trouble to make the table look nice, scattering tiny hearts on it. She was very thrifty; she could create a special atmosphere with very little, baking a cake or decorating lots of cupcakes. She insisted on inviting Kim's parents, Mike and Lyn, Kim's sister Sharon and Charlene, a friend of Kim's whose husband was away. She couldn't bear the idea of Charlene being alone. She loved gathering family and friends around her, organising everything. She always wanted people to be having a good time.

Also on 13 February 2013, she retweeted this plea from Lindiwe Suttle –

WEAR BLACK THIS FRIDAY IN SUPPORT AGAINST #RAPE AND WOMAN ABUSE #BLACK FRIDAY.

For three months I sleep with Reeva's ashes in my bedroom cupboard. They are in a long wooden box with a sliding lid marked with a simple handwritten label: REEVA REBECCA STEENKAMP 19/02/2013. I want to feel she's safe at home, close to us. I put Humphrey, her knitted doll, on top of the box of ashes because he was so important to her. She used to take him everywhere with her. One of Barry's aunts made the little jacket that matched his cute dungarees and bow tie. He's Humphrey Steenkamp. I remember the first time she went on an aeroplane alone, to Cape Town to stay with my parents, and I watched her board with Humphrey hanging out of the bag. Oh my word, I had tears in my eyes! I was just as apprehensive as she was because I didn't understand how the plane stays up there by itself and then this most precious thing of mine was climbing up the steps to board the plane with her doll ... I kept Humphrey. When Reeva had a baby I was going to give the baby Humphrey. Powder has chewed his feet a bit, but I know she'd find that amusing. He's a cat that eats jerseys. She chose Powder from the litter because he was showing off to her, doing backward somersaults and funny manoeuvres, anything to grab her attention.

At 9.45 a.m. on Monday 20 May 2013, we hold the Ashes Ceremony on Summerstrand Beach, officiated by Anglican minister Reverend Eddie Daniels. It is time to let her go. *Let her go* – that is a difficult thought to come to terms with during the half hour or so it takes to drive the twenty-five kilometres from our new house to the beach that Reeva loved. We have so many photos of her on the sand. This spot is where she posed for a fashion shoot for her first modelling pictures – kicking her heels aged fifteen in a beautiful white wedding dress, which remains Barry's most treasured image of her. It's a place where we're be able to visit her on her birthday and whenever we feel the need, now she's part of the sea. It is a beautiful, serene occasion. We have prayed for a fine day, and it is lovely, right from daybreak. The sea is also gentle and soothing. Accompanying Barry and I are Reeva's half-siblings from our previous marriages, my daughter Simone who is eighteen years her senior, and Barry's son Adam who is thirty-six; Barry's brother Michael, his wife Lyn and their daughter Kim; our great friend Jenny Strydom; Warren Lahoud, Reeva's former long-term boyfriend from Johannesburg, a wonderful, wonderful man; and several other close family members all join us to take leave of Reeva.

We make a little altar with an easel embedded in white rose petals and candles to display a black-and-white portrait of her as a model with a huge bouquet of roses. We are shielded from the big breaking waves by a barrier of rocks; occasional flecks of foam shower us and the roar of the ocean challenges the minister's voice as he tells us death is no more than sleep, a temporary absence until the resurrection. I say to the minister, who has all his flowing gowns on, 'Are we going into the water?' And he says reassuringly, 'It won't be that deep.' But even knee-deep, Barry can hardly stand up because of the pounding of the waves. We cling to each other. In the numbness of our grief, we feel the life force of the sea and that is strangely comforting. We all take ashes in our hands and spread the ashes into the water to send her off to the dolphins. We scatter rose petals as well and as we recite the words of the Lord's Prayer the waves come in and gently carry her away.

At the end we release a white dove to symbolise the release of her soul and then one hundred more white doves are released from crates along the beach. The minister concludes with the words – 'Go forth into the world in peace, be of good courage, fight the good fight of faith, that you may finish your course with joy.' I am overcome with emotion. Throughout the service the minister says words I know Reeva would have responded to. I feel her presence. The doves don't go away. They fly out with the ashes and then they swoop around in a circle and come back to us. That's magical. I take it as a sign that she will stay with us, that I will be able to sense her and talk to her all the time.

Reeva was very close to her grandfather, Barry's stepfather, who also had his ashes scattered in the Indian Ocean – at Bloubergstrand in Cape Town with Table Mountain in the background. She had his name tattooed inside her left wrist: Alec Luigi Serra. When she came back from filming the reality programme *Tropika Island of Treasure* in Jamaica, she told me that swimming with dolphins had been the best experience of her life. So I'm sure this is what she would have wanted, to be free and at peace with the dolphins. Pods of dolphins swim close to the shore at this beach and are often seen leaping through the waves. I know she would have wanted to be with them. She's out there with them now. I love thinking of her swimming with them, letting them kiss her, pulling her along, with a smile of pure pleasure breaking across her face. Whenever she used to snuggle up in bed with me I always thought she smelt of the sea.

I feel the ceremony is one tiny, tiny step towards . . . not closure – I'm not sure we will ever have that – but towards a point where we can consider moving forward with our lives. I treasure a stone picked up from the beach which Barry's niece Kim had inscribed for me with Reeva's name and the date.

On the night Reeva died an owl flew very slowly in front of my friend Jennifer as she drove back home from her restaurant, Peppa Joe's, just after 3 a.m. She's lived in the country for a long time and she's never witnessed an owl cross her path. The sight startled her; as she went to bed, she wondered if it was a sign and what it might mean, because in many cultures owls are associated with the other world and spiritual truth. Jenny and Reeva were very close – Reeva was like a daughter to her – and when she heard the news the next morning she realised what the owl had come to tell her.

Reeva was a beautiful spirit, always smiling and laughing. Kim, too, told me of a vision she had of Reeva with their grandfather, as if they were in heaven together, a good year before Valentine's Day 2013. Reeva was very close to her grandpa. They adored each other and she wrote him letters long after most people had given up the post for texts and emails. He had tried to call her two days before he passed on, and Reeva had not had time to return his call. When he died, she felt terribly guilty and upset that she had let him down and had not managed to contact him after that last call. She was never one to show that she was unhappy, but her distress about this overflowed in her cousin's presence. Kim reassured her that Grandpa would understand she had a busy life and that he would never hold a missed telephone call against the girl he loved so much. Later, Kim was at a retreat called Temenos in McGregor, near Robertson in the Western Cape. She was sitting in the serene spiral garden when there was a slight breeze in the trees and she looked up and saw Reeva and her grandfather walking hand in hand in the sky. Kim rang her in Johannesburg and said, 'I want you to know, I've had this vision of you and Grandpa walking happily with linked arms,' and Reeva replied, 'What are you telling me? Kimmy, are you mad?' And Kim told her it was her way of saying Grandpa was fine.

Now, she wonders, did the vision mean something else?

We are all asking these sorts of questions. You try to find some meaning in a situation that doesn't seem to make sense. You try and work out what life means and how it works. We need answers. What happened? Why? Was it somehow part of Reeva's destiny?

Reeva

Reeva meant the world to me. People don't know what to say to me because, in truth, nothing can bring a happy ending. I've learnt not to look for answers from other people. Only God knows my deep-seated pain. My parents gave me my religion and to me that is the most important thing. Although, with everything we're going through, I can't pretend it hasn't made a difference to the connection. I can't understand why this has happened to Reeva. I ask anguished questions. I drift away from my previous assumed beliefs, because it's hard to understand why something like this must happen to such a good child who has done no wrong and was a much-loved person. I'm not fond of going to church now, but that's not because I've lost my faith, it's because I feel uncomfortable seeking solace in the company of lots of people who recognise me. I've become a bit of a recluse due to the curiosity and scrutiny. But, deep down, I still believe in God. I'm just trying to puzzle out his mysterious ways.

Reeva and I had sat down and discussed what would happen if one of us died. We promised each other that whoever died first would send signs to the other to let them know they were okay. After Reeva died I went almost every day to spend time with Jennifer at Peppa Joe's. She and I would sit with a cup of coffee next to the fireplace which is used as an indoor *braai* or barbecue. Soon after Reeva died, things started dropping down the chimney. Objects dropped down

38

at home as well, and I take it as a sign. Reeva had a thing about feathers; she loved their delicacy and beauty. I started to notice little white feathers and I'd think: She's here. I'm sure there are lots of things you cling to in grief as signs that the person you have lost has not really gone away, and it makes me feel better to believe that her spirit is still with us, that there is some sort of communication and that she is telling me she is all right.

People write to me to say I should try not to be too unhappy because she *is* still with us and she wouldn't want us to be unhappy. And that helps. I love hearing people say things that suggest she still has strong desires and feelings, because she was a powerful personality. She can see that I can laugh. Soon after we lost Reeva, Simone chose to leave her job in England and move to stay with Barry and me. Like me, she's not very domesticated. Reeva was quite the opposite and Simone always says, 'She's watching us now. We're having too much to drink' – because she didn't like me having a drink. That's how she was! I always say at the age of twelve she became my mother and I became her daughter. She was so much fun, a real character – that's how I like to remember us, Simone, Reeva and myself, all three of us laughing together.

There'll always be the pain and the hurt now. That is never going to go away. I miss her so much. I can't phone her. I will never be able to talk with her again. I still have her number in my phone. I won't ever delete it. How could I just get rid of it? Barry also has her number in his phone and he has wanted to call it. She phoned me every Saturday evening and her father every Sunday evening for a long chat. Those times of the week feel especially empty. She was always concerned about us and wanting to take care of us. She would want us to be happy, I know that.

Missionaries in Ireland wrote to say they will be praying for her soul every day. A young artist called Etmáál van Jaarsveld, who is losing his sight to macular degeneration, painted a portrait of her as the tenth in his series of famous women as a personal gift to us. He was mad about her, and wondered about painting her. He talked about Reeva a lot to his mother and she said, 'Just do it.' He has captured her perfectly on canvas: her posture, her manner, her spirit. It is breathtakingly beautiful. When it was delivered if felt as if she had just walked into the house. An elderly man sent me R150 and wants me to buy a rose in Reeva's favourite colour, pale pink. People are kind.

Reclaiming Reeva

I think that the way you go out, not just your journey in life, but the way you go out and the way you make your exit is so important. You either make an impact in a positive way or negative way . . . just maintain integrity and maintain class and always be true to yourself.

Reeva Steenkamp, *Tropika Island of Treasure*
5 February 2013

At the end of Reeva's funeral, my brother-in-law Mike addressed the media gathered outside the Victoria Park Crematorium Chapel and said, 'Reeva stood against abuse against innocent women and that stand is more powerful now. She represented a world of strength, and people coming out of the church are stronger.'

That is the legacy we, her family, want to preserve. Since Reeva lost her life on 14 February 2013, she has been relentlessly referred to as 'Oscar Pistorius's model girlfriend', the 'slain glamour model and reality TV star' and as 'the deceased' by the judge and the defence team in the court proceedings. But Reeva was so much more than her day job and so much more than a beautiful woman photographed at red-carpet events next to a global sporting celebrity like the trophy girlfriend. She was as beautiful on the inside as she was on the outside. She was a wonderful daughter and friend, a personality who brightened so many lives, and she was also a law graduate and an exemplary citizen of modern 'rainbow nation' South Africa. She was not happy to sit back on her success as a model and TV personality; she wanted to use that platform to become a passionate voice for causes she felt strongly about and one day to play an effective legal role in raising the issue of abuse against women when she returned to a career in law.

Actress Phuti Khomo, who starred alongside her in *Tropika Island of Treasure 5,* summed this up perfectly in a letter she wrote to Reeva after her death which was published in the South African Sunday newspaper *City Press*:

You spoke isiXhosa but weren't as fluent as you were when

you were younger, so you planned on taking isiXhosa lessons so that you could communicate with your friends back in Umthatha and make them feel that they could still relate to you. It's that kind of selflessness that drew me so close to you. Many people don't know that the dream of becoming a model first came to you while lying paralysed in a hospital for months after a back injury incurred while horse riding ... You were educated, smart, beautiful, humble, kind, loving and understanding ... Every time I read the papers or watch the news, the story always starts with 'Oscar Pistorius' girlfriend'. No! I refuse to let that be your title. You are not going to be remembered as 'the girlfriend'. You wore many titles, some of which the world has yet to see. But the world will echo your name and remember you for who YOU are ... REEVA STEENKAMP.

It is a terrible irony that Reeva, who was super conscious of violence against women in South Africa, should now be famous all over the world as a symbol of domestic abuse. Her death has become a rallying point for campaigns. It seems painfully improbable that she met her untimely death on St Valentine's Day, the very date associated with romance and angelic winged cupids firing off love-inducing arrows; a day on which she had gone to cook a romantic dinner for her boyfriend, taking him a carefully wrapped present and card. Valentine's Day did not mean much to me or to Barry at our age. But for Reeva, it was a day she always noted with girl-ish excitement. She would want it to be a thrilling day for all her friends, like Abigail – a close friend from Port Elizabeth – with whom she'd annually exchange greetings: 'Happy Valentine's Day Sista!' She loved birthdays, engagements, weddings and holidays which are cause for cakes and cele-brations; she was good at choosing presents and cards and creating a sense of occasion. Now for us, and for her friends, 14 February will always signify the anniversary of her death. A day of romantic froth for others will always for us be a dark day accompanied by pain and suffering.

Reeva had started to use her visibility as a model to fight for causes that supported vulnerable people. Throughout 2012, she was a celebrity face of the Spirit Day anti-bullying cam-paign that her friend Mika Stefano coordinated in South Africa to highlight the fight against the bullying of lesbian, gay, bisexual and transgender youth. The South African campaign followed the lead of Oprah Winfrey and former basketball star Shaquille O'Neal in the United States. Reeva stood proudly among a multi-cultural gallery of celebrity supporters including Jamali singer Mariechan Luiters, models Lerato Kganyago, Celeste Khumalo and Tshego Seakgoe, former *Big Brother Africa*'s Lerato Sengadi, actor Anga Makubalo, openly gay personalities Sade Giliberti,

Bujy, Koyo Bala, Amstel, and DJ Olwee, and TV presenters Lalla Hirayama, Dineo Moeketsi and Sthembiso 'SK' Khoza to promote the cause. On 15 October she invited her friends to share a YouTube clip for the charity. 'Take a stand against bullying,' she urged. 'Wear purple. Please watch and share, friends! This means a lot to me! And wear purple on Friday! X.'

She was passionate about helping vulnerable animals too, often tweeting support in aid of the Ark Animal Centre – the leading rescue, rehabilitation and re-homing shelter in South Africa – and the Kitty and Puppy Haven – a rescue centre based in Johannesburg which takes in injured, abandoned, traumatised or abused dogs, puppies, kittens and cats. In the weeks before she died, she was photographed here, sub merged in affectionate puppies. **LOL they were attacking me with love** ☺, she tweeted.

When Reeva used to advise friends about relationship issues or difficult situations, her line was always, 'You deserve so much better'. Asked in an interview 'What's the dumbest thing a guy has ever said to you?' she replied: 'You'll amount to nothing without me.' The importance of self-worth was her mantra. As her close friend Kristin said to me, 'She was my biggest supporter if I felt down. I would always feel better after I'd talked to Reeva. There is a tendency when someone dies to put them on a pedestal, but with her it is true – she made a big effort to be a good friend, a good daughter, a good girlfriend. She went out of her way to engage with people, to be kind and nice.'

Keenly aware of the most violent end of the spectrum of abuse, she shared with her Twitter followers the shocking fact that in South Africa a woman is raped every four minutes and a woman killed by her partner every eight hours. She intended to use her growing profile as a media personality to highlight that situation and put her concerns into the practice of family law when she returned to her studies. This was not a token line. She had thought this through. In her short life she had been exposed to many vignettes of injustice and stories of ill treatment of women – which I will describe later in these pages – and she felt them personally. That was her big heart. She realised it was important to educate young girls to nurture their self-esteem from an early age, to encourage them to blossom as strong personalities so that they could not become vulnerable to aggressive or controlling behaviour.

It is a sad twist of fate that she had decided, shortly before she was shot, to speak out for the first time on this theme. She had arranged to give a speech to high school students at Sandown High School in Gauteng to urge the girls not to put up with being badly treated, demoralised or demeaned. She wanted to suggest that there is no obstacle in life that cannot be overcome. When she was about twenty, she was thrown from one of the horses Barry trained and broke her back in two places. For four or five weeks she lay in hospital with severely compressed discs. The doctors were uncertain whether she would be able to walk again. Slowly, slowly, wearing a supportive corset and enduring months of physiotherapy, she regained her strength and agility. Her notes for the talk were titled 'Placing Values on You' and she planned to tell the teenage girls about how she overcame difficulties in her life to become a model by reminding herself of her value to the world. 'I broke my back towards the end of varsity,' she wrote in her pointers. 'Learnt mobility again and made a massive life decision with regards to my career ... I was in an abusive relationship at the same time and all together these factors encouraged my move to [Johannesburg]. Despite my height disadvantage and the difficulty in general of breaking into the modelling industry, I put my head down and worked hard towards my dream ... it took some serious soul searching to remind myself of my value in this world.'

She was also going to tell the girls how important it is to be loved by others 'not for your physical appearance, but for who you are inside'. Her closing lines were typical Reeva: 'Be brave, always see the positive ... Go home and tell your parents, siblings, neighbours that they are appreciated. You will go to bed with a happy heart and an open mind for the future.'

She never got to give this talk. Can you believe it? Her publicist was preparing to drive to the school where Reeva would address the students when the horrifying news came through: Reeva herself had been gunned down by her boyfriend inside his home. In the end, Pearl Thusi read Reeva's speech out to the girls. She cried all the way through. She had to keep stopping to catch her breath. They were very close after *Tropika*, Pearl and Reeva.

Reeva felt for all vulnerable people. She went to school with a girl whose mother was a pioneering doctor who led a campaign for a more clinical approach to traditional bush practices such as circumcision. For young men, circumcision is seen as a rite of passage into manhood and those who have not undergone the procedure at so-called initiation schools in the bush are bullied and ostracised. But without sterilised instruments, the boys often develop severe infections; some of them lose their penis or even die. I remember when Reeva first heard about these things through her school-friend, she really felt for the loss of pride these maimed young men would have to live with. That was another vignette of life that developed her sensitivity to injustice. She presented a sunny side to the world, but inwardly she felt other people's pain. She was such a quirky, fun teenager who would randomly burst into song or dance or goof around, but inside she was a thinker and deeply compassionate. She always spotted the person in the room or the group who needed to be brought in.

Whatever happened in the small hours of 14 February 2013 will always stand as a double tragedy for two wonderful young people and their families. The lives of two gifted talents, two incredible role models, have been shattered. It's a cliché, but it is just *such a waste*.

I often think of what Reeva might have become. With that rush of bullets, he's taken everything away from her: her wedding, her babies, her career, her right to go to bed with a happy heart and an open mind for the future, her chance to make a difference.

Simone remembers her baby sister as the most amazing, passionate, compulsive, wild, crazy person who always did things at a hundred miles an hour. In retrospect it seems almost as if she knew she didn't have long. She had a short life, but she lived it to the absolute full. Her fellow graduate Angus Hayes wrote such a moving tribute to her. 'She was always kind and gentle and perfectly mannered – a true lady, without question,' he said, before addressing her spirit:

My dear Reeva, thank you for everything you did for me and for all the lessons. You were so busy after university fretting about becoming a success that you never stopped to see that you already are one. Forget riches and post-grads and titles. What better mark of success can there be than to add as much love to the world as you did? You were so special. You lived your life as you appeared to the world. You lived it beautifully. Our memories of you, this invisible light that you always gave to us so selflessly, will help us navigate our lives forever.

As a model, her dream was to be on TV and to appear in *Vanity Fair*, her favourite magazine. Ironically, both these dreams came true in response to her death. The magazine wrote about her fate in a piece illustrated with gorgeous images of her. She'd have loved that. And the first episode of *Tropika Island of Treasure 5* – a South African Broadcasting Corporation reality show where celebrities and members of the public compete against each other in an exotic location to win a million rand – was to air on Saturday 16 February, featuring Reeva alongside cool young South African celebrities including rappers Da L.E.S. and AKA, singer Mario Ogle and models Pearl Thusi, Phuti Khomo and Jay Anstey.

When Reeva and I spoke on 13 February she said she'd sent money to Barry and I for our cable TV to ensure we could see her in *Tropika*. She was proud of the programme. She'd loved spending those weeks filming in Jamaica in November in a happy bubble with her cast mates. She couldn't imagine a more surprisingly captivating experience than the day she spent swimming with dolphins. After her death, the network was under pressure to cancel the show. When the producers asked me for permission to show it with a special tribute to Reeva at the beginning of the series, I had no hesitation in saying, 'Yes, of course. Please air it.' I wanted to see her alive and laughing, see her happy and full of life. I told them what Reeva had said about the dolphins and that was why we were already thinking of scattering her ashes in the sea. Barry couldn't watch it, but I loved seeing her animated, and having fun, and I loved seeing other people revel in her company. That weekly vision of her on the show was lovely for me, every Saturday night for the ten weeks after we lost her.

When Reeva set off to Jamaica, it was all about enjoying the experience, not about winning the money. She was mature like that, an old soul. She was always one to stop to appreciate the moment and count her blessings. She didn't take any good fortune for granted. And she was absolutely true to herself on the programme. The cast called her 'Mama Bear'. There was a sweet bit when one of her fellow contestants said, 'I'm told even the Prime Minister has Reeva Fever.' He went on to compliment her, 'You're a sweet woman but always a formidable opponent. That's your beauty, that you can balance the two. Yes, I'm this stunning woman, but I'll also take you on.'

That was our Reeva: beguiling and strong-minded.

When it was time in each episode for the winner to sit on the throne, wearing the crown, and vote another contestant off the island, Reeva was always saved. Week after week, the others would say things like, 'This is a non-starter ... Babe, come through, Reeva. We can't imagine the island without you!' She was an almost ever-present cast member lighting up the screen and when finally, in episode 9, her turn came, she took the news with good grace. And that was when she said goodbye to me, when she sat against the palm tree on the beach with the sea behind her and talked about how your exit in life is as important as your journey. The episode ended as Reeva blew a kiss to the camera – a kiss that she meant for me. Frozen now in time. That was lovely.

Of course, when it was filmed, that snippet was part of the programme's format. One by one, as they are voted off, each departing contestant says their farewells to the island and the TV viewers. But it was typical that any speech Reeva would make could take on a deeper resonance. 'You literally fall in love with Jamaica. You fall in love with being in love with love. It's just one love everywhere!' she marvelled in the sentimental, girlish way we often used to speak together.

'I'm going home with, sort of, a sweet taste in my mouth. I don't have any regrets. I don't have any bitterness. I take home so many amazing memories and so many things that are in here [her head] and here [her heart] that I will treasure forever. I think the way that you go out, not just your journey in life but the way that you go out and make your exit, is so important. You either made an impact in a positive way or a negative way . . . just maintain integrity and maintain class and always be true to yourself. I'm going to miss you all so much. I love you very, very much.'

Rather like her teenage paintings, the way she chose to express herself seems eerie to us now, considering what was to happen to her inside the sleeping quarters of Oscar Pistorius's house. I later learn of a New York newspaper headline which ran: 'Slain model Reeva Steenkamp, two days after her surreal murder, resurfaced on reality television to deliver her own haunting epitaph.' Oh, there was such a fuss about people thinking the TV company were cashing in to boost ratings by airing the show days after she was killed. But, for me, it was just wonderful to see her beaming so vibrantly from the screen. For a precious half hour or so, it displaced the notion of her as the lifeless victim of the gruesome headlines.

Barry and I later received a lovely letter from Samantha Moon, the *Tropika* producer. She sent us DVDs of the series so that we would have those glorious images of her for ever.

Dear Mr and Mrs Steenkamp,
I hope that seeing your wonderful, vibrant daughter lighting up the screen brings you some solace. Reeva's zest and spirit, her sweet smile and infectious laugh, were so

evident. She was a sweet sweet girl, who I really enjoyed knowing. She spoke of you both so fondly even while on the island.

I'm not sure if you know, but Reeva watched the first episode with the entire cast and crew a few days before she passed on. It was a beautiful February day and we all sat in the sun teasing each other about how the first episode had come together. Reeva, ever polished and perfect, could not contain her raucous laughter and constant teasing of her cast mates. We all longed to be back in Jamaica, where every day was such an adventure. Reeva expressed to me that she was afraid in putting the show together Graeme and I would make it appear that she was mean, based on some stylised promotional spots we put together. I thought this was a preposterous idea, based solely on the fact that Reeva was the most loved cast mate which it didn't appear she realised until that very moment. She didn't know the effect she had on people. How her caring heart and nature was reciprocated with genuine affection. She touched everyone who knew her.

Samantha Moon, Sept 11 2013

It is a letter that I treasure. You cannot underestimate the healing power of letters such as that, from people who had really come to know the daughter I so cherished. Often, people hold back from writing to the family after a bereavement, but they shouldn't because letters bring immense comfort. They show other people have been touched by her, that they recognise her specialness, and that they care.

Reeva's big breakthrough in modelling was in getting the cover of the December 2011 issue of *FHM*. She had also featured in the *FHM* 2011 calendar. This cover-girl status, combined with her appearance on *Tropika,* was expected to be the lift-off for Reeva's profile after years of hard grind in the industry, working relentlessly to be polished and perfect, selling herself personality-wise to make up for her lack of inches. The minimum requirement for a model is 1.77m; Jane Celliers at ICE Models, Reeva's agency, admits she was being economical with the truth when she put 1.70 on her modelling card. But, by the end of February 2013, Reeva was going to reach household-name status by virtue of her own hard work as a professional model. That in itself was a measure of the character she was.

Jane told me recently the story of how she'd been approached by the *Tropika* production team to provide a blonde girl with a national profile to join the cast. Jane knew Reeva would be perfect so she said, 'I've got Reeva Steenkamp, a well-known model but not a household name. Please see her. She's wonderful.' Apparently Reeva walked into the audition and took everyone's breath away, as Jane knew she would. Even though the issues stemming from the incident when she broke her back meant that she was medically forbidden from doing some of the competitive activities – cliff-diving and so on – she won the part. That was so thrilling for her: they wanted her on the island for her personality. But there was one big proviso: for the next four to six months Jane had to take on the mission of making Reeva a household name. Jane threw her into any celebrity baking competition, any celebrity ballet class, any feature article in a magazine, any celebrity photo opportunity. The plan was that by the time she was on that island, all of South Africa would know who Reeva Steenkamp was.

That's the awful irony. When the first show aired, the whole *world* was aware of who Reeva Steenkamp was.

Limbo

On 14 August 2013, an indictment was served on the man who killed our daughter. It read:

The Director of Public Prosecutions for North Gauteng PRETORIA, of the High Court of South Africa, who presecutes for and on behalf of the State, hereby informs the Honourable Court that

OSCAR LEONARD CARL PISTORIUS

a 26 year old male, with South African citizenship (hereinafter referred to as the accused)

is guilty of the crimes of:

MURDER – READ WITH THE PROVISIONS OF SECTION 51(1) OF ACT 105 OF 1997

CONTRAVENTION OF SECTION 90 OF THE FIREARMS CONTROL ACT NO 60 OF 2000

COUNT 1 – MURDER – READ WITH THE PROVISIONS OF SECTION 51(1) OF ACT 105 OF 1997

IN THAT upon or about 14 February 2013 and at or near 286 Bushwillow Street, Silverwoods Country Estate, SILVER LAKES, in the district of PRETORIA, the accused did unlawfully and intentionally kill a person, to wit,

REEVA STEENKAMP

a 29 year old female

COUNT 2 – CONTRAVENTION OF SECTION 90 OF THE FIREARMS CONTROL ACT NO 60 OF 2000

THAT the accused is guilty of the offence of contravening the provisions of Section 90 read with Sections 1, 103, 117, 120(1)(a), Section 121 read with Schedule 4 and Section 151 of the Firearms Control Act 60 of 2000, and further read with Section 250 of the Criminal Procedure Act 51 of 1977 – Possession of ammunition.

IN THAT on or about 14 February 2013 and at or near 286 Bushwillow Street, Silverwoods Country Estate, SILVER LAKES, in the district of PRETORIA, the accused did unlawfully have in his possession ammunition, to wit 38 x 38 rounds without being the holder of

A license in respect of a firearm capable of discharging that ammunition

A permit to possess ammunition

Limbo

A dealer's license, manufacturer's license, gunsmith's license, import, export or in-transit permit or transporter's permit issued in terms of the Act;

Or is otherwise authorised to do so.

Wherefore upon due proof and conviction, the said Director of Public Prosecutions prays for sentence according to the provisions of Section 51(1) of Act 105 of 1997 against the accused.

THE STATE versus OSCAR LEONARD CARL PISTORIUS
SUMMARY OF SUBSTANTIAL FACTS IN TERMS OF
SECTION 144(3)(a) OF ACT 52 OF 1977

The accused was involved in a relationship with the deceased. The deceased chose to spend the night with the accused at his private residence. They were the only occupants of that residence at the time.

The deceased, a 29-year-old woman, was shot and killed in the home of the accused just after 03:00am on 14 February 2013.

The deceased had locked herself into the toilet cubicle, situated adjacent to the main bedroom. The accused armed himself with his 9mm pistol and through the locked door, fired four shots at the deceased. The deceased was wounded and died on the scene. The cause of death is given in the post-mortem report as

Reeva

'MULTIPLE GUNSHOT WOUNDS'

Some of the state witnesses heard a woman scream,
followed by moments of silence, then heard gunshots and
then more screaming.

    The accused said to witnesses on the scene, that he
thought she was an intruder. Even then, the accused shot
with the direct intention to kill a person. An *error in persona*
will not affect the intention to kill a human being.

There it was, the bare brutal scenario, in black and white.

On 20 November, we heard the news that Oscar had
been indicted on two further gun-related charges. According to the indictment, he had on a previous occasion
recklessly shot his gun (the same Taurus 9mm pistol he fired
at Reeva) out of the open sunroof of a friend's car while they
were out driving and that, on a separate occasion, he fired
someone else's handgun at Tasha's, a crowded family restaurant, apparently while admiring the weapon. The report
stated that for both alleged offences he could be charged
with public endangerment and damage to property, and that
he already faced a possible life sentence with a minimum of
twenty-five years in prison if convicted of the premeditated
murder.

The trial – *the State vs Oscar Pistorius* – was scheduled to start on 3 March 2014, in the Gauteng Division of the High Court of South Africa in Pretoria. The Trial of the Century. I was so apprehensive. The wording itself seemed to highlight the huge and surreal drama we found ourselves in: the state against its former golden boy and ambassador for Paralympic sport. As I saw it, I was going to face the man who killed my daughter and I would have to endure that with the world's cameras and reporters watching my every expression, gauging my reactions, monitoring my emotions. As long as we live, as long as we breathe, Barry and I will struggle to come to terms with Reeva's death. We are locked forever in unbearable grief. I'm a robust, strong person but it's hard to stop thinking that all the joy has gone from our lives. He has taken so much from her and us as a family. She was only twenty-nine when he killed her and she had just started talking about marriage and babies. I would have loved to help her choose her wedding dress. Barry would have been so proud to walk her down the aisle. We would have doted on the children that Reeva longed for. She was so family-orientated and would have enjoyed the enriching experience of motherhood, the pleasure of holding her baby and watching her baby grow, as I did with her. Her child would have been a beautiful grandchild for Barry and me, but he has taken that away from us all.

The one thing we hoped might help us through our lives

in the future is to know the truth of what had happened that night. That was all we wanted. We needed to know what happened that night between them. All we wanted were answers ... why it had to happen, why our beautiful daughter, the loveliest person who ever lived, had to die like this.

I was determined to face him. I wanted to look him in the eye.

At the same time, I was acutely aware that, whatever the outcome of the case, whatever justice was served for Reeva, there would always remain a giant void that can never be filled. Our advocate, Dup de Bruyn SC, who was introduced to us by Jennifer, prepared me for how I would feel. The trial would be very tiring, very stressful. It would be a punishing ordeal because we would have to immerse ourselves in the trauma and relive every single detail of that night when Reeva died, terrified and alone, over and over again. We would be stuck in the hellish bubble of time in which she met her death. While the lawyers debated technicalities ad infinitum, it would seem as if they had forgotten about our loss. We would sit through the state's case for murder and then we'd have to listen to the defence saying, oh no, it was just an unfortunate accident. I knew I'd find that difficult. But I wanted to be there for Reeva. It was important for me to reclaim my daughter. I didn't want her to be forgotten under the weight of all the forensic detail and nitty-gritty legal details and the drama of Oscar's self-absorption and self-pity. From what we'd seen since the day of his arrest, as far as he was concerned, it was all about him; this court case would be all about saving his life.

Before I spent my first long day sitting on those hard court benches – sandwiched between the inevitable media circus and the opposing legal teams, perched just behind Oscar himself, noting the grey patch in his hair, a legacy from the facial reconstruction he underwent following a 2009 crash on the Vaal River in a boat he was piloting – I prepared for what I knew was going to feel like a horrible exposure. Nobody has the right to try to get into my head. Nobody knows what's going on inside me. But I knew that the 'human interest' angle of reporting a news story meant many people would be scrutinising me for evidence of my emotions. I knew that the majority of people felt for me, and I appreciated that. When I visualised myself in court, I braced myself to be strong and decided I would try to get through it by withdrawing deep into myself and listening carefully to everything that was going on. I was there for a reason: I am Reeva's mother. I knew my presence would make Oscar feel uncomfortable. I was praying for answers. My strength and dignity would come from God and I had to trust that God would prevail and that justice would be done.

But it was not easy. Inside, I felt fragile and very vulnerable. I had to keep it together. Only after the trial would I be able to let go and grieve.

The ruling from Judge President Dunstan Mlambo to allow televisation of the proceedings added a further dimension. On one level, I felt the coverage could act as an exposure of important issues; on another level, I feared it might whip up opinion among a public ignorant of our intricate laws, and it might prevent witnesses from wanting to testify. Our personal tragedy had become the subject of such intense, global focus. The painful story of a beautiful young woman killed by gunshots, having tweeted about violence against women, had highlighted wider questions about our society. Whether Oscar Pistorius was found guilty of murder or culpable homicide or acquitted, the questions had been aired. Why is aggression towards women in South Africa so common? Why is gun violence so prevalent? It was the sort of discussion I often used to have with Reeva, who was horrified by the statistic that in our country a woman is killed by her partner every eight hours – the highest murder rate of women by their partners in the world. She was vocal about women and empowerment. When Oscar appeared in court for his bail and indictment hearings, members of the African National Congress Women's League held protests against crimes against women outside the building, marching with placards and drawing attention to two cases in session: the trial we must endure and another horrendous case already sitting in the courtroom next door against Thato Kutumela, who strangled and raped his pregnant eighteen-year-old girlfriend, Zanele Khumalo, in April 2011.

Barry wanted to be by my side in court but I insisted he stay at home. The doctors advised him to stay away. He remains broken by what has happened to Reeva. Two months after her death he suffered a stroke. One day after breakfast he opened a newspaper report about the upcoming trial and it broke him into pieces. He became delirious. He didn't know who he was or where he was. He couldn't speak and one side of his face collapsed. We rushed him to the doctor, who discovered a blood clot had reached his brain. After treatment, his face recovered, but he was not coping very well. The doctor prescribed him a pill to put under his tongue for those moments when his anxiety goes off the scale. I wouldn't let him attend court during the early stages because the high emotional stress could prompt another stroke, which might have killed him. I was prepared to go alone, with good friends and family supporting me. Our wonderfully supportive advocate Dup, a senior counsel or 'silk', proposed we go for one day of the trial and see how we went.

In the weeks leading up to the trial, the African National

Congress Women's League ladies phoned me and said, 'June, what do you need? Transport? Money for flights? Accommodation?' They swept in and organised everything for me. Jacqui Mofokeng, she could change the world! She's a wonderful, empathetic woman. She said it was the wish of the ANCWL, together with the South African Progressive Women's Movement, to help me attend court so that I could get some closure. She convinced me that I would feel stronger by the day if I could witness the trial and see justice at work. I told them I'd stayed previously in a comfortable guest house in the university area which I liked because it's small, a beautiful private house, and the owners are so sensitive and caring. A hotel is not private; it's impersonal and I didn't want to be on public display away from the courtroom as well. I wanted to stay somewhere away from the circus, somewhere I could be myself. The ANCWL ladies investigated the guest house. They approved it and they booked it for me. They also sorted out my flight from Port Elizabeth and organised a car which Jennifer was to drive as she was going to accompany me to court in Barry's absence.

And I have been so grateful for their support on every level. People said, 'What's this with the ANC Women's League? Is it political?' It's not political. They support me like a friend. They're like sisters to me. They removed all the anxieties about costs, and travel, and our general wellbeing. They wanted to come and visit Barry here at home while I was away in Pretoria and check he was well. Shoki Tshabalala, head of Social Development in Gauteng, promised to monitor our welfare. They were concerned about the effects of the trial on us. We are ordinary people with no resources to fund the many logistical and administrative repercussions of this tragedy. We have no experience of the law and legal procedures, but we are guided by Dup and words cannot do justice to the selfless and generous support he and his wife Truia have given us. They are incredible people.

We arrived in Pretoria on the evening of 2 March after a ninety-minute flight, Dup, Truia, Jennifer and myself. Pretoria is a very pleasant city, but I would not be driving through its jacaranda-lined suburbs, walking on its pavements dressed up in clothes suitable for a courtroom, were it not for the loss of my daughter. I had to try so hard not to cry because she was the reason I was there – but she was not there. I felt that acute sense of absence most when I went to Johannesburg or Pretoria. I'd only ever flown to Johannesburg to stay with Reeva. It was all horrific, but I had to be there for Reeva. People respected that. They said wonderful things to me. 'You're so strong,' they said. But I wasn't and I'm not. I've already collapsed a few times. It's as if I'm in purgatory. Sometimes I'm feel as if I'm going mad with it all. I had to consult a counsellor. I ended up crying and crying, but until the trial was over, I was determined to hold it in.

We printed a beautiful photograph of Reeva with her dates, 1983–2013, to pin on our jacket lapels and stick on the back of our court passes. That way Reeva would come to court with us every day. I had to think through what clothes I could wear to be respectful of the judge and the court – a smart black blazer, crisp white shirt and black trousers. I would wear the pearl necklace that Reeva saved up her pocket money and bought for me from her teacher's jewellery shop when she was twelve and an amethyst ring I gave her for her twenty-seventh birthday.

We went for one day, as Dup had suggested before the proceedings began. Monday 3 March was a miserable, rainy day. During the fifteen-minute drive from the guest house to the modern red-brick and stone High Court building in Madiba Street, I had to steel myself to attend this necessary judicial process on Reeva's behalf. My stomach was in knots. My heart was beating too quickly. I felt terribly on edge. The pouring rain had not deterred the media, who had encamped along the pavements flanking the High Court entrance to bring their audiences up-to-the-minute coverage of 'the Trial of the Century'. I walked through the tunnel of photographers and cameramen just trying to look where I was going and not trip over the tangle of cables that lay across the pavement. My steps through the gate and down towards the door that would lead us to Court Room GD confirmed the finality of my daughter's tragic end, leading me to the official process that would bring the man responsible for her death to justice – we hoped. It was difficult to bear, especially with the media frenzy on top of that. I hadn't anticipated the noise and claustrophobic presence of cameras, lenses, reporters, microphones, generators whirring on the pavements, people shouting: 'June, how are you feeling?' 'June, over here!' They were shouting my first name. It seemed so rude. I was on show. If I broke down or cried, everyone was watching me.

Even before I flew to Pretoria, I had had to adapt to this new lack of privacy. Regardless how I might try to go about my daily business and errands quietly, everyone recognises me. I've been in their sitting rooms on the TV coverage. People think they know me. Most of them want to hug me. And you can't refuse love, can you? It shows they care. Or worse, they stop me and *think* they know me ... from somewhere, but where? Can I hang on a minute while they work it out? I say quietly, 'I'm Reeva's mum.'

Present tense. I will always be Reeva's mum.

As I took my seat on the right-hand side of the front row bench that has been reserved with a placard for the Steenkamp family (the other side was reserved for the Pistorius clan), I knew what happened over the forecast three weeks would be difficult to sit through, but I took comfort from the fact that it would be a necessary evil that would help determine the truth of what happened to my child. It was so important I was there. It was important for *him* to know that I was there, that Reeva's mother, who gave birth to her and loved her, was there for her. This wasn't about the 'slain model' of the headlines. This wasn't about 'Oscar Pistorius's girlfriend'. This was, is, about my child, my beautiful daughter – the most wonderful, perfect child who meant everything to me. I really, really loved her. Barry as well. We were besotted with her.

From the minute she was born, I thought she was just beautiful.

Early Years

Reeva was born on 19 August 1983, at Greenpoint Hospital in Cape Town. It was eighteen years since I'd given birth to Simone and I was overcome with emotion, revelling in the glowing feeling that comes with producing an adorable little newborn baby. The midwives put her in the cot next to my bed and I couldn't take my eyes off her: the most perfect, beautiful child in the world. Friends came to see us in hospital and I remember hearing them whisper as they left the ward, 'Did you hear June say how beautiful she is?' They thought this was funny because my baby girl had one eye still closed and she was all purple and wrinkly, but she was everything that I needed to feel fulfilled: a precious baby who had dropped from heaven. I was so thankful to count all her fingers and toes. After Barry and I married in 1981, I became pregnant but suffered an ectopic pregnancy. The experience was emotionally distressing and I was gently advised that, even after a period of recovery, I had a reduced chance of conceiving again. Then I caught toxoplasmosis, a parasitic disease, from the cats. The doctor prescribed me drugs to treat it on the assumption that I wasn't pregnant, because the drugs can put an unborn child at risk. I didn't realise I was in the very early stages of pregnancy ... Can you imagine? Although I was overjoyed to be expecting, I worried to the day she was born that my baby would be blind, deaf or deformed in some way. I would put my hands on my tummy and just will this baby to grow healthily. I cherished her even before she was born. It was a very stressful period of time. And then this perfect little baby arrived. I wanted to call her Rebecca. When Barry came into the maternity ward he said he'd thought of a beautiful name for her: Reeva. A name from the Bible. So she was christened Reeva Rebecca Steenkamp.

Barry and I had been married for two years before Reeva came along. I was thirty-six, nearly thirty-seven; he was forty. We'd both been married before and had one child apiece: Simone, who I gave birth to when I was eighteen and still living with my first husband Tony in Blackburn, Lancashire, and Adam, from Barry's first marriage, who now lives in England. After two years of marriage, we were overjoyed to have a child together, we really were. Reeva made us a little family unit. Barry came to collect us from hospital in the Combi van. Just so that we felt like a complete family, he brought all my dogs. I looked out and honestly you could hardly see Barry for dogs. We carried Reeva home in a carry-cot, a contented baby. Those early months felt very blessed. I couldn't wait for her to wake up in the morning and start rocking her little cot. Barry was the same. Simone, too, couldn't stop picking her up to cuddle her. We were all just mesmerised by her.

In 1983 Barry and I were running the Burliegh Equitation Centre in the middle of Table View, a west coast suburb of Cape Town. We had 160 horses in livery and a little restaurant on site, which I ran. We used to stage show jumping events and organise hunting meets. It was a very sociable world and we are both gregarious people. Reeva came everywhere with us. We never left her. If we went out for supper, she came with us. She was part of our busy, sociable life. She was under the table in her cot in the restaurant two days after she was born. We lived in accommodation right in the middle of the centre. When you live with animals, you spend most of the time outside. We never had much money but there was no shortage of love and contentment. Our farm home was modest but cosy, with pictures of horses on the walls and lots of people in and out. With all the noise and bustle, Reeva could sleep on a clothes line.

I didn't go back to work properly until she was four. I wanted to spend every minute of the formative years with her. We had an open house. There was always a lot of fun going on with the young people who had horses with us. Claire, our next-door neighbour now in Greenbushes, was one of the girls on the farm. She was at school in Cape Town and she and her sister kept their horses with us. She used to come every Friday to our little farmhouse to sleep over with six or seven other girls. Michael and Lyn would drop off their daughters Kim and Sharon every weekend; they had their own room with us, and the cousins made quite a foursome with Adam and little Reeva.

I remember one day when I had to go out, I asked a lovely young girl called Michelle, who was studying for her final school year matriculation exams, to come and look after Reeva. She called on me only the other day, having dug out these sweet photographs of that day she spent babysitting. She'd been thinking about Reeva and suddenly remembered she had them somewhere. It was such a kind thing for her to do and I've put them all in a frame together to display at home. There are cute pictures – Reeva, aged two, smirking behind a pair of oversized sunglasses. Reeva sitting on the kitchen floor, covered in flour up to her ears, with the contents of a kitchen cupboard around her. Reeva, trying to eat toothpaste from one of twelve tubes I'd stored away after a bulk buy in Makro, the wholesale store. A real little character. Those were the days, hey?

At the age of two, she had her first pony and she was so proud to wear her little black riding jacket, tie and jodhpurs. She was best friends with a toddler called Melt, my friend Colleen Loebscher's son. They were inseparable. We used to feed them together, bath them together. They used to play happily for hours, zooming around on matching little red plastic pedal tractors that we'd bought for them at the Co-op where all the farmers go to get feed for their animals. Later she had a red-and-white Pro BMX bike, constructed by my best male friend, Allen le Roux Thomas. Barry has many talents but he can't put things like bikes together, so Allen assembled it for her. Reeva was so proud of it. We took a photo of her standing with her hand on her hip behind her new bike, looking very composed, as if she'd reached a new milestone of maturity. Poor Allen – he was to pass away just before his fiftieth birthday while riding his favourite horse, Beetlejuice, at Bloubergstrand. He simply dropped dead. That was terrible. He was so close to Reeva.

There were other interruptions to an idyllic childhood. When she was about five or six, Reeva had her tonsils taken out. My mother paid for the operation. We took Reeva home from hospital, put her to bed and gave her ice cream to soothe her throat as the nurses had suggested. She went to sleep and a few hours later woke up crying (thank goodness, because if she hadn't woken up she would have died). I hurried to comfort her and she projectile-vomited blood everywhere. We rushed her back to hospital. A friend, who was an anaesthetist, was on duty and called a surgeon immediately to close up the wound. Something had gone wrong and she nearly bled to death. It turned out the surgeon who had operated on her had been going through a difficult time in his personal life and every one of the five girls he operated on that day had to go back into hospital to recover. We were both there for her, hovering over her hospital bed, very anxious about how she'd pull through. But she bounced back.

In 1990, at the age of seven, she went to her first show, the Western Province Horse Society Summer Show in the middle of the racecourse at the Cape Hunt and Polo Club on the cutest little skewbald pony, Pinto. She won seven rosettes, including a rosette for Best Walk. I don't believe the rosettes were for her competence. A week beforehand, something had dropped on her fingernail and it had died and was about to fall off. She had all the judges enthralled with this wobbly fingernail. They were so taken up with her and her engaging character that they gave her all these rosettes. Her charisma, not her pony skills, won her the prizes.

After Pinto, she graduated to Ziggy Stardust. When Ziggy had a foal and couldn't be ridden for a while, she moved on to sedate A-grade ponies – calm, well schooled and so ancient one died in the paddock of old age. We just wanted her to be safe. I went hunting every Sunday with lots of friends. We all had horses together. It was a happy, social scene. Reeva wasn't as absolutely mad keen on horses as us, but she loved life at the yard, particularly following the vet around. One day we'd called him to attend a sick horse and she watched him inject the horse in the rump, her big blue eyes out on stalks. Just after the vet had left, we were looking for Reeva when we heard her screaming. Barry had all these plastic syringes and bits and pieces lying around the tack room and she'd taken one, filled it with I don't know what, and squirted it up poor old Pinto's bottom. She was playing the vet, and nearly got kicked by two hind hooves for her effort!

It was a very happy time. She had a wonderful, free child-hood playing with friends and roaming around the stables, always at the heart of what was going on in our lives. She went to fancy-dress parties. I made her up like a little angel, with wings and rosy cheeks and lipstick and glitter. We always had a party for her birthday. And every Christmas, Barry would dress up as Father Christmas for all the children at Burliegh. She would never ask Santa for dolls and Barbies, she would ask for a garage for her car collection. She wasn't girly, more of an outdoorsy tomboy. She was always mad about cars. Year later, when she was being officially introduced by

FHM as a new cover girl, I laughed when I read the accompanying interview. She'd said, 'People assume I'm of the princess variety. But the only Barbie I owned growing up was one that came with a horse. Needless to say, Barbie was burnt at the stake by my Lego men. I only ever had guy mates growing up – and I'm grateful for it!'

She displayed a nurturing nature from an early age. Kim, who is eleven years older than Reeva, reminded me of the occasion when she'd been rude to me and her parents, Michael and Lyn, drove her over to Burliegh to apologise. 'I sat in the car distraught,' recalls Kim. 'And little Reeva came out and said, "Don't worry, Kimmy, it will be fine." It was amazing – a five-year-old consoling a brat of a sixteen-year-old teenager who had come to apologise to Aunty June!'

When she was eight, we took her to church to be baptised. My parents had instilled their Protestant faith in me and I wanted her to grow up a strong Christian. Barry, too; he has always read his bible. It was such a big thing for her. When the minister, following the traditional set service, asked her: Do you believe in God? Reeva shouted her answers at the top of her voice in case anyone wasn't listening, 'Yes! OF COURSE I do!' She was a big personality from the start. She had natural warmth and charisma. We treasure a photo of her holding hands with Barry from that day. She's dressed for the occasion in a white dress and pale pink jacket, with long white socks and pretty shoes, her long wavy hair tied back. On the back she's written proudly, *Me and My Dad*.

Her grandparents adored her. They had a special relationship with this little *laat lammetjie* of ours, particularly Barry's stepfather, Alec Luigi Serra. He was an amazing man, an Italian, and he loved her to bits. They didn't have much money, her grandparents, but they put money into a Post Office account in her name. They wanted to do that for her. Someone said to me that even though she died early and we only had a short time with her, we all probably got more love from her than some parents and grandparents get in a whole lifetime. She was a strong character. My other daughter is too. Even though we are going through bad times, we can laugh at things, finds ways to be happy and stay strong. I've always told my girls that you need a really strong sense of humour in life.

In 1991 we uprooted from Cape Town to Port Elizabeth to ensure Barry had work. It's difficult to make ends meet in the horsey world, let alone make money. We always struggled financially, Barry and I. We always had to muddle through. When you run a large livery stable, you have to feed the horses in your care and pay your grooms to help muck out and exercise them, but often owners don't meet their bills. You can't stop feeding and looking after the animals just because their owners don't settle their bills on time, or pay up at all in some cases. We had a lot of problems with that. People just didn't see paying for their horses' care and keep as a priority; but we needed to live. To make money in horses, you need to breed, and we didn't have baby horses. So it became tough to keep the Burliegh Equitation Centre running as a going concern for us in Cape Town, although we loved our life there and all our friends. Barry found a niche training horses in Port Elizabeth so we left, heading east along the Indian Ocean coast to PE, a calmer, sleepier city. In fact, Barry went six months in advance, and people thought we might have separated. Finally the three of us moved into accommodation at the Jockey Academy while Barry ran his horses at Arlington racecourse. Before long he had about fifty horses in training and about twenty grooms who lived in lodgings at the racecourse with their women and children and babies, and often quite extended families. Barry and I were used to working together in Cape Town, and I wanted to continue that dynamic with Reeva, of course, in tow, so I set up a spaza shop at the racecourse. For fifteen years I ran the shop, a sort of informal convenience store selling kilos of flour and rice to supply the day-to-day grocery needs for these workers' families.

When she wasn't at school, Reeva was often at my side in the spaza shop. One of the old black gentlemen said the other day he remembered her warmth and kindness and her big smile. She grew up with all those mommies and daddies and babies and children. I was friends with all these women as they went about their domestic chores. Every day we'd chat. They would share their family stories with me and also some of the horrendous dramas that they or their loved ones had endured. That made an impression on Reeva and I have no doubt contributed to the way she felt about the treatment of women as she grew up. One of these women had a daughter the same age as Reeva and the two became friends. When the girls were fourteen, Reeva confided to me that this girl was crying because she wanted to go to school like Reeva but her mother was being forced to sell her for R7,000 to an old man – an old man who could have had Aids or anything. It was sickening. This poor black girl cried and cried and said she just wanted to be like Reeva, and that broke Reeva's heart.

This tale is deeply shocking and I can't apologise for making it sound like an everyday occurrence because there were *always* stories of people treating their daughters as a possession that they could make money from. When you're the mother of a daughter of that age yourself, you feel the outrage very deeply. Reeva and I heard it all: a father locking a girl in a room and letting a series of men rape her for money; mothers who were forced to take their young girls to walk the railway line, a well-known area for prostitutes. Reeva took all that on board, all these young girls whose childhood had been brought to an end abruptly and sordidly, who were used by their own parents as a means to bring in money. She is okay, now, that fourteen-year-old girl who just wanted to go to school like Reeva. She went through all that but she met and married someone who cares for her and looks after her.

But that was later.

For Reeva, the most dramatic aspect of moving from Cape Town when she was eight was a change of junior school. I remember taking her to see Sister Anne at St Dominic's Priory. When Sister bent down and said, 'Well, Reeva, we've got lovely clothes in the second-hand shop for you ...' Reeva started crying. 'Mommy, tell her I don't wear other peoples' clothes.' That's how she was! Sister Anne is now a very gentle, frail old lady, but she was quite formidable when Reeva first arrived at St Dominic's. On one occasion, it was Reeva's birthday and I'd brought in a cake for her to share with her class, but she decided she'd rather spend the day with me. She just walked out of school and made her way back to our place at Arlington – that's an hour's walk through the Bush. One of the teachers was sent to fetch her. Back at school, Sister Anne scolded her: 'What did you think you were doing? Walking through the Bush? You could've been chopped into tiny pieces. Tiny pieces, my girl!'

St Dominic's is an independent, co-educational Catholic day school and it was very good for Reeva. Founded in 1900, it is situated in beautiful manicured grounds, surrounded by woodland near Walmer, a garden suburb, with lots of playing fields. The school motto, *Veritas* – Truth – is in keeping with the tradition of the original nine Dominican nuns who founded the school to perpetuate the line from Psalm 117: 'the Truth of the Lord that endures forever'. I was brought up a Protestant, but the Catholic faith was a good grounding for Reeva. St Dominic's is the sort of school where everybody knows everybody; no one is just a number like at a government school. She thrived in that atmosphere and she stayed there all the way through high school too, as Trinity High School merged with St Dominic's and shared the premises. It wasn't cheap. Fees today range from R16,600 per annum for pre school to R39,260 per annum in Grade 12, the final year of high school. There is a new headmaster there now, but the philosophy of personal development and emphasis on charity and helping the underprivileged persists. In the headmaster's office I noticed on a recent visit a lovely sign on his pinboard about every child being a seed fallen to earth who will germinate and grow and ripen and bear fruit.

In this environment Reeva's natural human kindness took on a wider dimension. 'That child didn't have to be taught Christianity; she had it inside her,' insists Nombulelo Ntlangu, who taught her Xhosa, one of the official languages of South Africa distinguished by its click consonants:

'For some people, it's a new thing, learning to work in this diverse world of cultures, but that child knew how to do it instinctively. She was an old soul. She was so clever, she never saw colour in a person. All our students had to do three languages – English, Xhosa, Afrikaans – but that child never differentiated. She fitted in every group. That fascinated me. She never made a fuss or showed an awareness of colour or wondered why I, her Xhosa teacher, could be a class teacher in the way some other children did. She worked with people across colour – Indian girls, coloured girls, black girls. She was prepared for our new modern world when she was young.'

Today I take great comfort in the way the teachers remember Reeva so clearly as someone who always had a presence. After she'd moved to Johannesburg, whenever she'd fly down to PE to visit us she would wonder how her old teachers were and always tried to pop in to see them. Since her death, they have been generous in sharing their memories of her with me. Oh, I've learnt a lot! There was the sister who always referred to Reeva as 'the mannequin'. And the male teacher who had just got divorced and opened up to his class asking if any of them had a sister his age. Apparently Reeva had shot up her arm and declared, 'I'll get you a date with my sister Simone!' That was her, always willing to help others.

The teacher wore a toupée, so poor Simone insisted their date was somewhere nice and quiet.

I've had a good laugh with Di Cowie, her games teacher, reminiscing about the time she was asked by Sister Anne to come and fetch Reeva after her doomed birthday walk across the Bush. Di was bowled over years later when, long after Reeva had left school, she was sitting in her car outside the bank and Reeva – back for a visit to PE – strolled over and gave her a hug. 'As a student, she always greeted you warmly, "Hello, ma'am," even if she was rushing past you in the passage, and that always brightened my day,' said Mrs Ntlangu.

St Dominic's Priory truly celebrated individuality, which was good for a girl who was brought up virtually as an only child. Barry and I had made a conscious decision to send Reeva to a school that made a virtue of this Rainbow Nation of ours. The annual school magazine was full of snippets about the diverse talents of pupils – singing, charity work, sports achievements, engineering projects, you name it. There are lots of photos of Reeva as a finalist in a modelling competition, a semi-finalist in an event sponsored by Liquifruit, being hailed for her 'unique sense of style' and 'fashion flair'. During Operation Charity Week, she led the Grade 9 effort:

'I personally feel that the grade nines gave it their all to really spice up the festivities. We decided that a Wacky Day would do the thing and it certainly made everyone feel relaxed and comfy in their natural state of mind. (No offence to be taken!) We raised a substantial amount of money and feel great that we helped with a really good cause!'

In 2001, her penultimate year at school, she was Captain of Rosary House with Mark Francis and signed off with an effervescent end-of-year report:

'Competition among our three houses caused sparks of passion and tremendous spirit to ignite a wildfire of enthusiasm and incredible sportsmanship and commitment among all team members! As Head of Rosary for 2001, we are proud and most definitely confident in saying that our team put up an incredible fight this year and proved that they could certainly work side-by-side and smile, though faced with disappointment and defeat . . .'

Her maths teach, Selma Lourens, tells me Reeva herself was never aware of her beauty. 'She was a magnetic personality who lit up a room with her smile and she was just so sincere,' she said. 'She was so natural. She never mentioned her modelling success, even though it must have meant a lot to her. When we heard the awful news of her death, a lot of press came to interview those of us who had known and taught her. The students became enthralled by her story and the memories she inspired in all of us. They said, "Ma'am, please when we die, please will you talk about us like that."'

But there is also a poignant aspect to these conversations. As Mrs Ntlangu said to me, there was always, in amongst that sense of urgency and *carpe diem* philosophy that Reeva displayed, the sense that she somehow knew that her time on Earth might be short. It was perhaps why she felt the need to keep coming back to Port Elizabeth to update her teachers on what she was doing, as though she had some impulse to give it all some permanence and fix herself in the minds of the people she felt had played the greatest part in her life.

Reeva always appreciated what her teachers did for her. She was mature like that. She realised her passage through school was a two-way dynamic. 'I remember when she brought in a clipping from her first big modelling job,' Mrs Ntlangu told me. 'She was still that humble Reeva. She didn't want praise, she wanted to know how it was at St Dominic's. You know, sometimes I think people know when their time on Earth is going to be short. Not many kids would come and update us with their activities or careers, but she came to visit us.'

After the events of 14 February 2013, St Dominic's held a minute's silence for Reeva at the Past Pupils' Dinner. For the current pool of young schoolchildren, it was quite an ordeal when the news hit the headlines that South Africa's squeaky clean superstar role-model athlete had killed his girlfriend – a girl who had once worn the same navy-and-gold-striped uniform blazer as them, who had sat in the same classrooms and prayed in the same chapel. TV vans had taken up a vigil on the road outside the school's electronic gate; there were cameras on roofs overlooking the private grounds. The school eventually had to say enough is enough, and they asked the press to move on. It was a disturbing intrusion of 'the real world' for young, impressionable students. 'Some of the teachers who'd known her were very distressed,' Greg Stokell, the headmaster, told me. 'We held a special assembly to celebrate Reeva's life and also to introduce to the boys and girls the notion of the harsh reality of life, because that's what her death represented. No one knows how many days they have and Reeva was a role model in the way she made each day count.'

She certainly loved school. From an early age she was driven to learn and improve herself. She liked to do well. She liked to take pride in her progress. She was a people pleaser by nature and that meant she always wanted to do her best for her teachers. In her box of childhood keepsakes, she stashed her Certificates of Merit for English, Afrikaans, Biblical Studies, Creative Writing (she won a cup for that too), Science, general Outstanding Work, Swimming Safety, you name it. One report from March 1998 gives her class average as circa 45 to 50 per cent. Reeva was awarded 5/5 for behaviour and the following marks: Accountancy 85 per cent,

Biblical Studies 81 per cent, Afrikaans 80 per cent, Science 78 per cent, Maths 79 per cent, Biology 88 per cent, English 77 per cent, Xhosa 94 per cent, Geography 82 per cent. I was so proud of my daughter. How could I have produced her? I was never one to focus at school. I spent more time being sent out of the classroom than sitting in it, but Reeva was the opposite. She was extremely conscientious. She wrote reams of poetry, some of which was printed in the school magazines. As well as being an outgoing child, she had a sensitive side. Here's a poem called 'Footsteps' she composed for one of the school annuals. The innocent words she penned now take on a haunting echo:

Tiny footsteps quake the home . . .
Fleeing over, under and far away.
Bigger footsteps quake the infant . . .
Raging, into, over and through.
Mother's footsteps quake the heart . . .
Loving, caring, weeping, mourning.
Daddy's footsteps quake the cells . . .
Nodding, pleading, wishing, hoping.
People's footsteps quake the graves . . .
Placing tiny footsteps over, under and far away.

In another, called 'My Garden', she ends with the verse:

Reeva

I sit and think, the willow holding me
And watch the breezes give life and take
There in my garden, I can see
Each life is at stake.

Reeva never missed a day of school. She never said she felt unwell. She would be standing by the car waiting for me to take her to school. I was the one who was always late. I was called in by the sisters and told I was ruining my daughter's life by being late each morning. It takes me time to get going first thing – my other daughter's the same – but Reeva wasn't like that at all. From an early age she was highly driven, highly self-motivated. Some people might call this borderline Obsessive-Compulsive Disorder, but really she was just inclined to be extremely organised. This was a girl who would have her school bags ready the night before, her room tidied. Every week she would take things out of her wardrobe and re-shelve things, rearrange her clothes. She was scrupulously structured and organised; she liked everything just so. She would never leave a piece of clothing on the floor. Neither would I, for that matter, but for a child and a teenager she was unusually meticulous. She always tried to please her teachers, but she went through one phase when, totally unlike her, she went off the boil in a few subjects. Sister Anne called her in and asked her what was going on,

With Barry, in happier times

Reeva as a beautiful baby

Two of the photos taken by Reeva's dear babysitter, Michelle –
precious memories

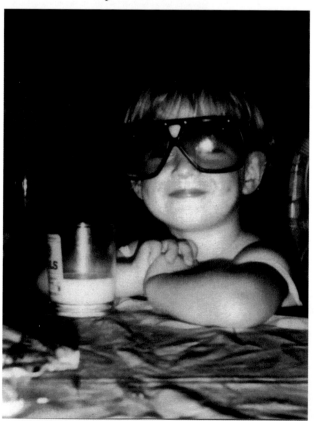

Reeva's love of animals – especially horses – never wavered, not even when she broke her back aged twenty. Here, she's learning to ride on Pinto the pony

Always a sporty girl

Aged eight, just before her baptism. Reeva had proudly written on the back of this photo *Me and My Dad*

Turning into a teenager – but still with her love of animals

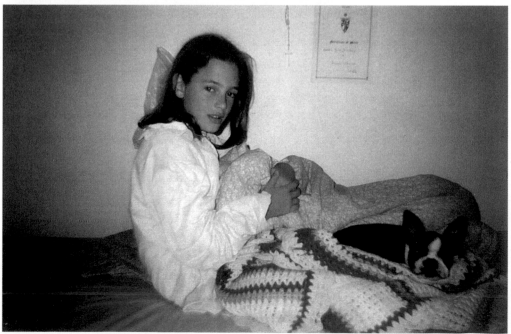

Reeva was such a committed, intelligent pupil

The early days of a
modelling career

With her friend, Garth, on the night of her high school matriculation dance

We were incredibly proud of Reeva getting her Law degree – she made a stunning graduate, here with fellow student, Angus Hayes

A photo from the beautiful wedding shoot on Summerstrand beach, taken when Reeva was only fifteen and where her ashes are now scattered

and then Sister Anne called me and said, 'I think she's in love with this boy in school . . . '

Hard work was something we all understood in our family. My mother and father met when they were both working in the same factory. As a family, we all have a strong work ethic. I was born on 26 September 1946, in Blackburn, Lancashire. I was an only child because my mother had such a difficult birth with me that she couldn't get pregnant again. My parents never communicated a sense of sadness that they couldn't have more children. They gave me a wonderful time growing up. We lived first in a terraced house on Heys Lane with a pub at the end of the street, and I went to the little local school. I remember my early life as idyllic, even though it was spent in an industrial town. You know the 'four thousand holes' in the Beatles' song 'A Day in the Life', the one that starts 'I read the news today, oh boy'? That was said to have been inspired by a newspaper report that caught John Lennon's eye about Blackburn's four thousand potholes. My parents worked long days, 5 a.m. to 7 p.m., so after school I had to go to Granny up the road. Every holiday we went to London and saw a show, or we travelled to Wales or Scotland. As an only child, I was allowed to take a friend. They were thoughtful like that, my parents. They doted on me. I didn't have to cook or do any cleaning or domestic chores, they just created a little cocoon of happiness around me. I hunted every Sunday. I did eight years of ballet and riding; Saturday was ballet day, Sunday my day with horses and ponies. I had friends who had horses and I used to ride with them.

My mother was a determined lady. She had always wanted to be a nurse but her mother wouldn't let her, so after working all week in the factory she spent every weekend in the infirmary, working for nothing, studying in her spare time. She was eventually able to take her exams and become a nursing sister. Then she was happy. She loved her role as a sister at the hospital. She also hankered after a house with cows in the paddock next to us, so we moved to a bungalow in Langho, a small rural village about five miles outside Blackburn in the Ribble Valley. I had been very happy at my lovely secondary modern school in Blackburn but when we uprooted I had to move to a new school in Great Harwood. You had to fight to stand up for yourself there. On my first day, a girl smacked me in the chops, but by the time I left I was the best fighter in the school. Once, after I had danced with a boy on whom another girl had a crush, I was attacked by this girl and her friend. They grabbed me by the hair, but I responded by flooring them.

My father was awarded a medal from the Queen for thirty-six years of service in a factory with a royal warrant which had made guns and equipment during the war. My parents were working people and they instilled in me the idea that you have to provide. That was the environment I grew up in and to this day I love waking up, getting dressed in the morning, going off to work – even if it takes me a while to get going! Otherwise why bother to get dressed? I've always been a business woman, not a stay-at-home lady of leisure. I've run shops, cosmetic counters, laundrettes, pubs, catering businesses, stables, you name it.

When I was sixteen, my mother asked what I intended to do when I left school. 'Oh, I don't know,' I said. 'But don't worry.'

'Oh, I'm not worried,' she was quick to reply. 'I've booked you in to start work at Boots the Chemist the day after you finish.'

I left school at sixteen and got a certificate in hairdressing. I was married at seventeen to Tony Cowburn, who was a toolmaker, and Simone was born when I was eighteen. They used to have a Saturday lunchtime dance at the Mecca and I met my first husband there when I was about fourteen or fifteen. We emigrated to Cape Town in 1965. Tony used to visit South Africa for work and stay for three months at a time. It was good business for him and he was doing well. He came back to our little house in Blackburn one day and said, 'Why don't we go and live in Africa?' I had a primitive vision of what that might entail. What, elephants in the street and tigers marching around? But I thought anything was better than being in the same small industrial town I'd known all my life. I'd had a lovely childhood, but now I thought I wanted to see some of the world. His enthusiasm for the thriving business opportunities and the beauty of South Africa was contagious, so we left.

I arrived in Cape Town with baby Simone, and discovered very quickly that Tony seemed to have lady friends all over the place. My parents came to stay with me out here. And then my mother – still a nursing sister – told me she'd never wanted to upset me, but she knew he was friendly with all the nurses at her hospital as well. Anyway ... the marriage got me here and then I left him. I just picked up my child with nowhere to go, no work, nothing, and how I survived I don't know, but I did. I think that's why I am strong and resilient today. I couldn't even boil an egg then. I spoke to my ex-husband on the phone the other day when he called to speak to Simone and he said, 'Do you still have the tin opener?' My parents had done everything for me and I'd never learned to cook. When I was first married I used to go to the supermarket and stock up on tins of food. It must have been terrible.

As a single mother, I held down about three jobs at once to make ends meet. We lived in this little room in Greenpoint, full of fleas. I met another girl who was also alone with a child and we moved in together to reduce costs and help each other out. We survived. At one stage I was working in hairdressing by day and in a smart restaurant club in the evening. We used to wrap the kids' Christmas presents in newspaper. Simone was a lovely little girl. She enjoyed reading and burying herself in books. My parents had always had lots of books too. We had next to no money. To get by, I tried my hand at every sort of advertised job you can think of. I once went for an interview to be a dental nurse and the dentist told me that every Saturday they provided treatment for abscesses. He explained how they cut into the gum, drained the abscess and there was often a lot of blood. These were the patients I'd be tending. 'Don't worry about me, I'll be fine,' I said, keen to get the job. On my first morning he reminded me that, should I feel queasy, I must go out of the room. Well, I was out of the room the whole morning. We had one of those conversations – 'This isn't working for me, it's not working for me either' – and that was the end of my apprenticeship as a dental nurse.

My parents fell in love with South Africa too, and moved out to Cape Town permanently. I went to stay with them for a while, but that didn't work. You can't go home to your mother and father! So then I got my own little place. I worked for a surgeon for eight years, and then I moved into cosmetics. Stuttafords department store introduced Christian Dior products and I got the job to run the counter. I loved it. Simone and I survived and she had a wonderful, happy childhood. I made sure of that.

I still had my love for horses and kept my own horse at Milnerton Riding Club, and that's how I met Barry. He was born in Cape Town to a family with an illustrious racing heritage. His uncle Cookie Amos was a brilliant horseman and top trainer in South Africa and his other uncle, Stanley Llewellyn Amos, was for many years the top jockey; he won almost every big race in the country at least once. The two uncles brought him up because his mother divorced his father and in the aftermath he went to live with them. Stanley Amos won no less than 2,507 races – which was, at one time, a world record. Barry loved the world of racehorses. He hardly ever went to school. When he did go, he'd give tips to the teachers and get away with murder. He's intelligent, very intuitive, and he speaks Xhosa, English and Afrikaans. As a youngster he had worked for Cookie Amos and then became a private trainer to Alfie Heyns in Cape Town.

We went to the movies on our first date and saw *Chariots of Fire*. We clicked immediately. Before Barry, I'd had a boyfriend who was very wealthy and suave, but Barry was my wild man of Borneo. He was big and tall and had a beautiful figure; he'd just lost twenty-five kilos and could even boast a six-pack in those days. Five days after our first date, Barry asked me to marry him over dinner – and I said yes. That was our first dinner together and it was so sweet; he went to a lot of trouble and cooked me fish, knowing I was vegetarian, and had candles on the table and a bottle of wine. He was a gentle, strong man and the epicentre of fun at the equitation centre; we loved the same things, horses and so on. He phoned his mother and told her he was getting married and I phoned my mum. We had to phone our exes to get the court papers and we were married five days after the proposal – just ten days after our first date. Simone was thirteen when Barry came into my life. I'd told her I was thinking of marrying him and she, being a melodramatic teenager, said, 'I'll kill myself!' I said, 'No. You'll be fine.' She stormed off to live with her father but rang me after a week and said, 'Mummy, I want to come home.' So she did and Barry has been 'Pop' to her ever since.

When I first met Barry he was doing amateur racing. He did so well I suggested he take out his training licence. I didn't want him to get old and look back and regret that he'd never given it a go. I said, 'You must go and do that. That's what you want to do. That's what you love.' He took out his licence, and he's been breaking in and training horses for forty years now. It's been up and down in terms of financial stability, but Barry has sound expertise. He's known for being one of the most experienced racehorse conditioners on the circuit and for being a master at steering unsound horses back to competitive fitness.

Two years ago, some big owner took him out to the tune of a couple of hundred thousand rand and we didn't have money set aside, so Barry had to close his stables. The owner had a 'carte blanche' agreement with Barry that he never honoured. He never paid him a single rand. It bankrupted Barry, wiped us out. It was an emotionally wrenching experience for him. He's always loved his horses and gained satisfaction from watching them develop, and then suddenly he had no horses, no means of earning a living or filling a day. He didn't know what to do with himself. He sat there, depressed, smoking, and then this happened . . . It was blow upon blow because Reeva, of all people, was so proud of seeing him in his racing environment. She took such interest in his racing world. She loved helping him in the yard, hearing about his prospective winners. She loved the excitement of the races after seeing all the days of training and conditioning that goes into getting a horse ready to compete. In her box of favourite things, she kept a cutting of a photo of Barry at Arlington with the race card of his runners. In the years when she was at varsity she spent a lot of time in and around Barry's yard. A lot of her friends were here. It was a busy, fun atmosphere. Abigail, an assistant trainer who became her close friend, always described Uncle Barry's yard – as she called it – as a 'halfway house' with lots of interesting people coming and going, and Barry would be sitting behind his desk, this big man with this big grey beard, smoking like a trooper, a glass of whatever by his side – and he never had his shoes on.

But I'm jumping ahead of myself.

When Reeva was twelve, she became my mother and I became her daughter. Barry now says he realises she became his mother too. She was always concerned about us. She truly was an old soul. I felt she'd been on this Earth before. She used to give psychology lessons to my friends and to hers. She always knew what to do. Samantha, who was at St Dominic's with her from the age of ten or eleven, agrees she was wise beyond her years. She was the sort of friend to whom people who didn't ordinarily 'open up' about their feelings found themselves confiding and telling her everything that was going on in their lives. She understood how the world worked and how you had to work hard and make sacrifices to pursue a chosen path. Reeva was always aware that money did not grow on trees in our garden. When she was about nine or ten, she won R900 on the horses and took it straight into school and approached the bursar to put it in for her school fees! And sometimes she would tell me to behave because she was 'goody two-shoes', as I used to remind her affectionately. She gave Barry and me a hard time! She would tell me what clothes to buy. I'm quite conservative and I can pick out a nice enough outfit, but she had *style*. She knew how to put things together. She was good at the handbags and trimmings. The first thing she ever bought me was a string of real freshwater pearls. One of her teachers had a shop with pearls and she must have saved up her pocket money for weeks to buy them. She always wanted me to look nice. Later, she'd buy me clothes and I'd look at them and think, hmm, and put them in the wardrobe, but when I'd try them on I'd see they were perfect. She had a good eye. My friends relied on her judgement too – Jenny used to send her out with a credit card to buy her clothes and perfume.

When Reeva was thirteen, we moved from the country to Kruger Street in Mount Pleasant. It was more suburban, but I wanted to leave the farm and live close to the shopping malls so she could meet her friends safely, go shopping, do the things teenage girls do, meet and chat. At about this time Barry and I separated. Some things in life you like to keep private and this is one of those phases – but there wasn't any huge drama. We just weren't getting on living under one roof. We never divorced, or intended to divorce. We simply needed our own space, and we muddled along quite happily being a family to Reeva under two separate roofs. I grew up an only child and I had lived for a long time alone as a single mother with Simone. I've always been an independent spirit, so I wasn't worried about moving with Reeva to my own place in Miramar, a pretty duck-egg blue cottage on Abbey

Road – just outside the gates to St Dominic's Priory and not far from Barry in Mount Pleasant. My parents had died and left me a bit of money, so I could afford to invest in a little house. By then Simone – who, like me, had married for the first time very young – had two sons, Christiaan and Nicholas. They also lived in Miramar, just around the corner, and the boys went to St Dominic's at the start of their schooling. They're lovely boys. Reeva was officially their aunt, but she was only a year or so older than Christiaan, who is two years older than his brother, so the three of them grew up together almost like siblings in our extended family.

Reeva was heartbroken over our separation, she truly was. It was a difficult time for her because she loved both of us. There is no good age for a child to experience their parents' split, but twelve to thirteen is a particularly vulnerable age I think. It was tough on her. She would have liked for us to live together under one roof as a family. She did realise there were problems, but she was devoted to both of us. She never gave us trouble; she was never rebellious or gave us cause to worry. She never took sides. Throughout her school and varsity years she'd live with me during the week and she often stayed with Barry at the weekends. She kept up the feeling of family among us. We always celebrated all our birthdays together and came together for Christmas, but Barry and I would continue to live separately for another fourteen years. Neither of us looked for, or found, anyone else. We were just happier living independently. We saw each other every day, because I worked for him running the spaza shop and I had the contract to do the catering at the racecourse for meets. And if Reeva was involved in something, we'd go together to watch her. And Reeva being Reeva, she was always involved in plays or music or cabaret at school, or modelling competitions outside of school, so she kept us tightly glued. She was always the glue holding us together.

Years later – in October 2008 – Reeva brought us back together for ever. Reeva, the Superglue. My cottage in Abbey Road was in a little townhouse complex close to the grounds of St Dominic's Priory (a historic plot of land which was originally Emerald Hill farm, then a hotel and pub before it was bought by nine pioneering Dominican nuns in the early 1900s). It was considered a safe part of town. We lived there, Reeva and I, until she finished varsity at the age of twenty-two. In 2008 she was twenty-five and living in Johannesburg when I phoned to tell her the lady next door had been broken into and we were having a residents' meeting in someone's garage to discuss security. She insisted on flying down to attend the meeting with me; she wanted to be reassured about my security. She always worried about me living on my own. That same night of the meeting, we came home, shared a lovely supper together, and then she went to her room and I went to mine. At 1 a.m., the Jack Russells started barking frantically. I got up and went to take a look and as I did the security alarm went off. Through the grille covering the kitchen door I found myself face to face with an intruder who was attacking the door with a crowbar. He wasn't deterred by my presence. Having already got the huge lock on the big security gate open, he and his accomplice were pretty determined to break in. He didn't even look at me as I warned him off; he just carried on trying to force his way in. In the yard outside the kitchen door I had a small mushroom-top *braai*, a mini barbecue or outdoor cooking grill. He picked that up and knocked the entire window through – security bars, frame, glass and everything, and then two of them came running into the lounge.

Reeva shouted out to me, 'Mummy, quick, come into the bedroom!' and we locked ourselves in. We both instinctively did that, steeling ourselves behind the locked door. I looked at her, and she looked at me, and we were like two ghosts, shaking from head to foot. We were paralysed with fear. We'd secured the door, but it was just an internal lock, and we didn't know if they'd break the door down, or what they were going to do. I was terrified they'd rape her. I was cursing myself for calling her in Johannesburg and involving her. I didn't want her to be here, experiencing this horror. It was truly terrifying. Every mother will understand when I say I wasn't worried for myself; I was petrified her life would be over if those drug addicts rampaging through our property got hold of her. For fifteen minutes they ran around the house, turning it upside down. They took my laptop. Reeva had a brand-new laptop, but thankfully she'd put it under her bed when she went to sleep. Suddenly it all went quiet. The men had left. The security team arrived and close behind them all the male neighbours who'd agreed in the meeting earlier that very evening to come if they heard an alarm sound.

It horrifies me now to imagine how similar this experience was to what must have happened to Reeva. We weren't in a toilet cubicle, but we were behind a locked door in the middle of the night. Having shared that experience with her, I imagine just how terrified she must have been in the early hours of 14 February 2013, to bolt herself, alone, behind a secure door. I've no doubt of it. She locked herself in the toilet of Oscar's house that night out of pure terror.

The next morning Reeva said to me, 'Mummy, you can't sleep in this house by yourself again. I'm going back to Johannesburg tomorrow and you're going back to my father.' She was right. I couldn't stay there by myself; I was too scared. She packed my bags. As always, she took over. Barry borrowed a truck and took all my stuff the very next morning. So, after fourteen years, I had to go back to father dear ...

I've always loved Barry, and it was Reeva who brought us back together. In doing so, she saved our marriage and she saved my life. A week later the guy returned to my empty little cottage. The alarm was switched on inside the house so he assumed I was inside. During his first attack, I'd eyed him through the security grille and said the thing you should never say. I couldn't help myself. I was outraged that he felt he could just invade my home, and when my daughter was there, and I'd shouted, 'I'll get you at some stage. I'll find you – I don't care how.' I'd seen his face. They don't like that. They normally wear balaclavas. So he came back for me. And he must have been incensed to find me gone, because he chopped all my bamboo blinds to pieces and then he left in the drive, as a warning, his big panga machete – the huge scythe they use in the Bush which can chop a head off.

Reeva and I both had to have therapy after that intrusion. She went back to Johannesburg and saw someone. She was so upset she wrote a letter to the local newspaper, saying how sad it was that we must live like this even in Port Elizabeth and that criminals could get away with their disgusting behaviour. On top of her strong sense of right-eousness, she became ultra-alert to security. 'I would rather be too careful and aware than have someone we love injured or harmed in any way,' she wrote. The experience scarred her. I resisted treatment for a while but I went a bit weird.

You get paranoid, you know. If I left home I thought that everyone in the street was going to stab me. But I did feel safe, back with Barry. And Reeva felt comforted knowing we were together. In the long run, it's been good for both of us, especially now. We've never stopped loving each other. We support each other, you know.

In her teenage years, Reeva was friends equally with boys and girls. There was Samantha and Gwyn who shared her love of horses; there was Benjamin, whose father complained about the phone bill because his son spent hours on the phone to her. There was Angus, and Garth, who directed lots of cabaret and musical shows. She went to her high school matriculation dance with him, dressed in a royal blue silk halter-neck crop top and long skirt; her wavy brunette hair down to her waist. She and Garth could both turn on a creative temperament. Garth implored Reeva to play a particular role in a show he was directing. When the day came and he showed her what she had to wear, she said, 'I can't do that. I'm not wearing that!' – and she just walked. 'I'm leaving!' she declared. 'I'm firing myself!'

She was very focused on all her activities. She studied at school and did her homework. She always had a rehearsal for a production of some sort going on. She loved spending time with her friends. She'd be up at the stables with Barry and the horses or helping me out in the spaza shop or with the race-course catering. She also loved modelling. She was busy, busy, busy. She started taking an interest in modelling at the age of fourteen. It was a fun thing, doing fashion shows and being part of something that was separate from school and university life. She was so beautiful, you know. She had thick dark brown hair, clear luminous skin, freckles, and naturally rosy full lips. You can see Barry's big blue eyes and you can see me. One day she asked me if I really was her mother and whether she was adopted. I don't know what that was about! Even when she was a professional, and posing for *FHM*, she said the main appeal of modelling was the fact you get to dress up and play pretend. When she was fifteen she posed for a competition in the local newspaper wearing a black leather jacket. Her first experience of a serious fashion shoot came the same year at a wedding fair, when she posed in several dresses and looked absolutely radiant with her hair half-pinned up in a sleeveless white gown on the beach at Summerstrand – the same spot where nearly fifteen years later we were to hold her ashes ceremony. She had already perfected that innocent yet coquettish sideways glance towards the camera. Even then a tremendous spirit comes across in the photographs. Mark West, who took the pictures, announced she had 'that X factor'. He said she changed a room when she entered; not in a loud, showy way, just in her radiant serenity. Barbara

Robertson, a fashion editor who noted her at a Futures competition, commented on how she had a sort of commercial look about her as well as a lovely freshness and way of letting the camera reach into her soul.

Modelling was something she discovered for herself, and I respected the way she went about making it 'her thing'. She was never self-absorbed. We didn't have the sort of bathroom in which she could spend hours in front of a mirror. For her, it was all about looking healthy. When she was that age, she used to give me a list of what she'd eaten every day because she did not want to get fat. So I had to sit and listen to what she'd eaten for breakfast, lunch and dinner. It was her own little OCD thing, and I listened patiently because I knew it was part of her ambition to become a model. She wanted to look after herself. I've always been a vegetarian or a 'fishatarian' – because when I was younger I was obsessed with not eating animals. It was a romantic kind of thing: I gave up meat, then chicken, eggs and fish, and I ended up very sick. The doctor explained that if you've grown up eating animal protein, your body continues to need or expect it. But I only ate fish when I carried Reeva in my womb and she was never crazy about meat. I suppose, if your mother is a total vegetarian, you're just not exposed as much to meat. She certainly had meat now and again. I didn't try to influence her. She was always going to have her own ideas. As a mother, you have to let them develop their own way. More than anything, she was into fish and cakes. Banana cake was her speciality. She loved baking. Unlike me at her age, she was perfectly capable at cooking and she enjoyed trying out recipes. She wanted to be competent in everything she did.

With the modelling, it wasn't so much being in the lime-light that she enjoyed but the feeling that she was following a path that marked her out as someone who was going to do something special with their life. She wanted to make some-thing of herself. Nobody listens to the bag lady with her trolley full of all her clothes, do they? She wanted to be somebody notable so people would listen to her. There was a tendency, I felt, in some of her early pictures for her to be over made up. She didn't need make-up. She had strong colouring with her blue eyes, dark hair, freckles and incred-ibly clear skin. I think she was more beautiful without any make-up. And she had a positive choice of clothing. She always had the handbag, you know. It was in Grade 10 that Mrs Ntlangu became aware she was blossoming. 'I looked at her one day and noticed how that child is growing and I said, "Reeva, I think you should do modelling. You've got a very beautiful face." When she walked, she had nice upright shoulders. Reeva smiled and said, "Thank you, ma'am" – always so gentle and full of courtesy.'

Reeva worked for my friend Jennifer at the restaurant she

owned back then, Buffalo Bills. Jennifer had her front of house because she charmed customers. She could talk to anyone as if she were one of their own. I remember once in our kitchen, Reeva was sighing to Jenny about her maths homework and Jenny just said, 'Darling, you are so lovely and gorgeous, you won't have to do maths for long. You are going to be a famous model, Miss South Africa!'

When she was sixteen or seventeen, Reeva wrote to Craig Native, the designer who was raised in the ghettos of South Africa at the height of apartheid, and asked him to design a dress for her. That was quite a bold thing for a schoolgirl from Port Elizabeth to do, but he responded to her in similar vein. She kept the letter in her box of special memories. 'I would gladly like to design you a dress . . . obviously,' he replied. 'I am a fan of non-conformity . . . like yourself. I know you're in PE. We'll make it work somehow, though? We'll innovate.'

After school, Reeva wanted to study law. She enrolled in the four-year Bachelor of Laws degree at the Nelson Mandela Metropolitan University which has a campus in Summerstrand, Port Elizabeth, close to the beach The course covered all the different kinds of law – constitutional, family, criminal, human rights, labour, company, administrative, property, insolvency and so on. Within the first few days of class she met Kristin, who was later to become a good friend to her in Johannesburg, too, when they were both graduates. Kristin reminded me that at this stage she used to think Reeva resembled the actress Liv Tyler with her long brunette hair and pale, pale skin. Kristin said that, compared to her, Reeva seemed quite streetwise. She was also an earnest student and drifted towards the more studious types in the class; she attended lectures, took notes, always got good marks. She used to say to Kristin that one day they'd set up together and have offices like Ally McBeal in the American TV legal comedy drama.

During her final years of varsity, we nearly lost Reeva. She was up at the stables with Barry when she fell from a horse and broke her back, severely compressing two vertebrae. After little Pinto, Reeva had moved on to bigger horses. From the age of ten or eleven, she would ride for fun with friends like Samantha and Gwyn and help Barry by exercising some of the racehorses he had in training. She was very comfortable around horses, but you can never protect against a horse having a freak stumble or reacting in fright to something unforeseen. I was busy shopping at Makro, stocking up on bulk purchases for my spaza shop, when Barry phoned me and said, 'Now I don't want you to get worried, but Reeva's fallen from a horse. I think she's okay.' The girl who had given her this horse had reassured her that it had already been worked for the day, and should be quiet, but as soon as Reeva was in the saddle, this horse took off and threw her over its

111

head, bang, on to the ground. Her face was full of sand; she had blood coming out of her mouth. Barry took her straight to the doctor – not the hospital, the doctor. You're not supposed to move people with potential back injuries, but the ambulance here comes four hours after you've called for it, so you have to make a judgement about what you're going to do. Barry made up his mind and took her to our doctor. The doctor X-rayed her back and said it wasn't too bad, but insisted she go immediately to hospital. At the hospital they diagnosed two vertebral compression fractures. They put her in traction, using weights around her neck to relieve pressure on her spine, and the specialists admitted they were unable to say for certain whether she'd be able to walk again until the day she was ready to stand up.

You can imagine how frightening this was for all of us. For four months, our energetic, vivacious daughter was confined to a hospital bed, flat on her back, unsure how fully she would be able to resume her independent life as a student. This was followed by months in bed at home. It was an anxious time as she felt frustrated about falling behind in her studies and potentially wrecking her modelling ambitions. She had worked hard to attain straight A grades to get her to university and she wanted to get the most out of her law studies. It was incredibly traumatic. I sat by her bedside every day as if she were in a coma. Privately I'd cry, fearful that she would never regain her mobility. Not knowing for so long how bad the injuries might prove to be was very wearing; Reeva cried a lot, lying in bed. She developed an infection from being bed bound, a nasty case of shingles, and lay there a very sorry figure with this pale white face and big red blotchy marks everywhere. When she had visitors, though, she'd make light of her situation and lie there making wise-cracks.

There was such anxiety in the build-up towards the first time she tried to stand up that she fainted. She'd been lying down all those weeks . . . we were all watching her take to her feet . . . and then she falls down, her legs giving way beneath her. I was thinking, oh my word, maybe she is never going to walk again. Slowly, oh so slowly, she did regain her mobility. The doctor said she was very lucky. But she would never be able to ride again. In Johannesburg a few years later, her friend Kristin wanted to learn to ride and thought Reeva the obvious friend to ask to come along to support her. 'She really wasn't keen,' Kristin recalls. 'She was scared, too, and out of the two of us I was always the one more scared about everything.' With one of her main passions forbidden to her, Reeva channelled more energy into pursuing modelling as a serious option.

Reeva carried that setback around with her for a long time mentally and physically. She was determined to make each day count. She left hospital wearing a made-to-measure surgical corset, a sort of plastic supportive cage which she had to wear every day for months. She had regular physiotherapy and endured a lot of lingering pain, but she worked hard to regain her fitness and perfect posture. After she succeeded in gaining her law qualification at varsity, the first thing she bought was a therapeutic bed. She paid a lot of money for a really good mattress.

Over the next few years she studied during the week, but at weekends she'd spend a lot of her free time up at the stables. She was unable to ride, but working life for Barry and me centred around the horses and the race meeting schedule, and Arlington racecourse was the epicentre of our social lives. In her early twenties, she became close friends with Abigail, who was working as an assistant trainer based at Arlington. I was running my little shop and Reeva would be there sometimes to help me in the spaza or with the catering on race days, or she might be loitering around with Barry. Of course Barry and I were still separated then and his life revolved around his racing community. He lived at Little Chelsea Farm, otherwise known as Barry's Barn on the Farm, a building in Sardinia Bay which had about fifteen bedrooms. Inside, there was a partition so that Reeva could stay on one side over weekends, and Barry and his apprentice and other trainers and jockeys lived on the other side. There was a huge communal kitchen and living space and when the venue staged a double race meeting – full Friday and Sunday race cards – all the jockeys would stay over. Abigail and Reeva used to have some good parties!

As a mother you're not always privy to all the details of your daughter's youthful partying ways, but I've since learnt from sharing memories with Abigail that a typical weekend would see these apprentice jockeys and Reeva all pile into Abigail's little car. They'd go to Toby Jo's and this dodgy place called Redemption in the old post office in Port Elizabeth that held serious raves. They were big into their weekend raving, but good clean raving. No drugs, no drink. She used to come home sopping wet because the raves had a party cannon that shot out plumes of foam. Abigail was always the designated driver and never used to drink. Reeva hardly ever drank either. The pair of them usually drank tea. The girls had very different lives during the week – Reeva at varsity, Abigail working long hard days in the yard – but they reconnected each weekend to socialise and confide in each other about boys and things. They had the kind of easy friendship where you just pick up exactly where you left off and trust each other implicitly.

At the age of sixteen Reeva had started seeing an apprentice jockey, Wayne Agrella, who was her first serious boyfriend. They were together for six years, and eventually lived together.

Another apprentice had asked Wayne to ask Reeva to ask Abigail to come out to supper because he liked her ... It was that kind of scene. They were all young and crazy and having fun. And these young jockeys had to be so disciplined to make their weight that they were moody. They had a sort of bad-boy swagger that made them attractive. They were on a constant diet, sweating off the weight and living on lettuce leaves, and that left the heavier ones particularly grumpy, but they were also the heroes – the glamorous guys who risked everything to deliver wins for the trainers. Off duty, they were fun to party with, but they weren't good romantic partners for the girls. Reeva loved Wayne. She used to cook him steamed fish and vegetables and make him healthy salads. She gave him a photo and wrote on the back, 'I will always love you. Forever + ever my babes. Even if we are a million miles apart. Reeves xxx'. And Wayne loved Reeva. He had two winners the day she gave him the photograph and he rode them in her name. He always said the best thing about being a jockey in Port Elizabeth was meeting Barry Steenkamp's daughter. 'She's exactly like her dad,' he said. 'He'll give his last rand away before he worries about himself.'

For jockeys, their job is their life. It's a tough, competitive, intense schedule. Their mood depends on their ratio of winners to losers. There are more bad days than good, that's how it goes. Reeva mentioned in her notes for the speech she was due to give to schoolgirls the day she died that she had once been in an 'abusive relationship'. That was just shorthand, we're sure, for being in a relationship she knew wasn't good for her. She was never physically hurt, but she was probably on the wrong end of words that belittled her. Was she cheated on? Yes, that's why she left him in the end. They were both young, strong-minded people. But she loved Wayne. He was her first love, sweetheart love, and she wasn't mature enough to walk away until her heart was broken. Relationships are never smooth and easy, are they? As soon as you start loving someone, you start hurting as well because you have expectations of a relationship. Reeva was very proud. She was never, ever, ever one to air her dirty laundry, but she knew she had to move away as soon as she finished her degree course to escape the relationship and regain her self-esteem. Port Elizabeth was too small a community to have hung around in. She was always someone who'd plan ahead carefully, and she looked to make a break.

Reeva had carried on modelling through varsity. In 2004 she was a finalist in the *Weekend Post* Faces of the Future competition. A year later she was a finalist in the *Herald* Miss Port Elizabeth contest. After her transformation from brunette to blonde, she won the Face of Avon competition and as part of the winner's prize flew to Johannesburg to participate in a shoot and enjoy a brief immersion in the world of talent agencies. While she was there, she walked into ICE Models and spoke to Jane Celliers, the agency director, who booked her straight away. At least, that was the story that became family lore. What I didn't know at the time was how hard Reeva had to knock at the door. Jane told me recently that when Reeva had first dropped her an email from Port Elizabeth, explaining that she had won the national Face of Avon competition and wanted to pursue a career in modelling once she had finished her law degree, her standard response had been to ask how tall she was. When Reeva replied, she said, 'I'm so sorry. You are absolutely beautiful, but your height is a problem.'

Reeva being Reeva, this was not good enough. Soon afterwards she telephoned Jane saying she was in Johannesburg, she was coming to the area, please would she meet with her. 'She walked through the door and it was love at first sight,' Jane said. 'Wow! This is Reeva.' Jane acknowledged that yes, she was short by modelling standards, where the minimum requirement is 1.77m, but she had something very special about her. 'She was probably 1.68 or 1.69 but I rounded it up to 1.70 on her modelling card because I was on her side,' Jane told me. 'She was extremely beautiful. Within a few minutes of talking to her I could see that, as well as having that irresistible girl-next-door look, she could be glamorous or natural. She was very versatile. In person, she was matter-of-fact. There was no bull with her. She was outgoing; she had this vivacious, throaty laugh. And I could see from her hair, her skin and her nails, that she looked after herself very well.'

Jane warned her that at twenty-two, she would be embarking on a modelling career a lot later than most girls and that because she had concentrated on her education beforehand and because of her restricted height, she would have to work incredibly hard in the business. She was not built like a coat hanger on stilts. She would need to make sure her personality won through; she would have to shine in every casting. Garments do look better on taller, longer models, so she couldn't do the catwalk shows though she could expect to be invited to do the odd private boutique show. Mostly she would have to concentrate on editorial and catalogue work, plus TV commercials.

Reeva was prepared to give it all she had; she was excited and, as a small-town country girl, she was also a bit nervous about moving city and living a different kind of life. In her last year of her law degree course, she had dyed her hair blonde because it became clear she would get more modelling work that way. She was quite tactical about presenting herself with a sellable look. She planned to make a career out of modelling for as long as she could before returning to fulfil her law ambitions. In a way, it meant there was no dilemma. She didn't want to look back one day with regret and think, 'If only I'd persisted with modelling . . . ' There was an ideal timeframe. She knew that as she neared thirty there would be younger, prettier girls coming through. She and Abigail forged a strategy. After varsity, Reeva was going to move to Johannesburg and Abigail was going to London. As Abigail divulged to me, 'Reeva wanted to go to Johannesburg, make her stamp, make her money; I was going to go to London to work and get my British passport. Then we were going to come home and go with our thirties. That was our plan.'

Barry and I both felt nervous about her going to Johannesburg, but it was so exhilarating for her. When she had first learnt to drive, she had a little beat-up old car which her father bought her, because that's what they all want at that age. Barry said that sending her to Johannesburg in the beat-up car would be like sending her naked. He scraped together to get her a new car and bought her a brand-new little Spark. He just wanted her to be safe.

I'd had Reeva at home with me for twenty-two years when she spread her wings and flew off to pursue her own life. We had an arrangement to have long weekly phone calls: Saturday was my day, Sunday was Barry's. Just as I'd written in the letter for her eighteenth birthday, I had no worries about her on many levels. I knew she was sensible, intelligent and very together – but I did still fear her heart might get her into trouble.

Reeva went off with Abigail's words ringing in her ears:

'Keep grounded. Remember where you come from. Don't get lost. Don't get caught up in the cattiness. Be true to yourself. And forget about these riffraff jockeys! You need to go to Johannesburg and you need to find yourself a nice man, not a boy, a man, who is going to look after you and treat you well.'

Johannesburg

In 2006 Reeva packed a single suitcase and moved to Johannesburg to follow her dream of being a model. If she had stayed in Port Elizabeth and carried on with her law studies, she would almost certainly be alive today. That's a difficult fact for Barry to absorb because he always said he would prefer her to continue in law and not take up modelling as a career. In fact, whenever he spoke to her on the phone, he'd end the call by asking her when she was coming home. It was his sign-off, almost a joke, but not really. In the last few months of her life he even started calling her and begging her to come home. It was as if he had a feeling in his bones that she would come to harm in the city-slicker world she inhabited more than a thousand kilometres away from the slower pace of her home town. But I understood why Reeva felt the need to move away and take up an exciting opportunity. You have to let your children find their own vocation. Just as I urged Barry to get his licence and try his hand at racehorse training when we were first married, I supported Reeva in her desire to pursue modelling. I was so proud of our beautiful daughter. What mother wouldn't be? And I've always been one to encourage people to give things a go.

We didn't see Reeva for a year after she moved to Johannesburg. She found city life difficult and slightly alienating when she first moved there; she had to work hard to find a sense of belonging. Johannesburg is all about work, all about money. In comparison Port Elizabeth is a calm, sleepy coastal town which most young people leave behind as they go off to a big city – Johannesburg, Cape Town or Durban – to earn a living and forge a career. I think she felt that if she came back for a short break, it would be hard to throw herself back into her Johannesburg whirl again. And, of course, she was afraid she might be tempted to go back to Wayne. She really loved him, you know.

I missed her so much that first year. When she came back for her first visit home, Barry and I both went to meet her at the airport and there were a lot of screeches and laughs, a real carry on. We'd all cry with laughter. I always kept her bedroom ready for her in my little cottage, but she often came and slept by me. On that first trip back, she came to the races to support Barry's horse and of course I worked there too. When the races finished, all her friends came in. Wayne was the last to arrive but they kissed each other and she said, 'I still love you, you know.'

Modelling gave Reeva a path and a direction. It is a world where image is everything, and that can make for a very competitive, judgemental environment. Each girl is selling an individual 'look', and it's hard not to take it personally when that 'look' is rejected. Equally, each job is so hard to win that praise from your peers is rarely forthcoming. Reeva's experience of modelling in Port Elizabeth was not so much about competition as about camaraderie. It wasn't a profession; it was something she did for fun. As her mother, I knew she was in safe hands with Jane at ICE Models in Johannesburg and I knew Reeva had not underestimated the fact that modelling at national level required serious focus. To be ready to forge a career as a model, rather than prepare for an occasional shoot or assignment, she had to get into shape, and she had the brains to realise she was going to have to work on it. It wasn't going to just happen. She could see what she needed to put in, in order to get well-paid assignments out of it. A lot of girls don't see that. They're not driven enough. But Reeva understood her shortcomings.

Before a model is cast for an editorial or TV commercial shoot, a brief goes out to the talent agencies describing the job for which models are to be auditioned. Thanks to Jane's warnings about the need to push her personality, Reeva's trump card was that she always made a huge effort to study the brief. If a client wanted a girl to appear in, let's say, a TV coffee shop commercial in the guise of a corporate worker, Reeva would go out of her way to interpret the brief. She would figure that the client might not have the imagination to see what she'd look like dressed as an office worker if she turned up in the normal model outfit of leggings, flat shoes and casual top, so she would attend the casting looking polished and professional above and beyond. She always went the extra mile to get the booking. In between jobs, she worked extremely hard to maintain herself. She ate well and drank three litres of water a day. She went to the salon to keep her hair in tip-top colour and condition, and her nails camera-ready. She went to the gym to hone her body. She loved the whole business of skin care. A few years later, in 2008 or so, she would decide to have implants to boost the number of jobs she would be eligible to audition for. She underwent quite a transformation, but it was for the purpose of achieving her goals. Whereas some models would consider an *FHM* cover the pinnacle of a career, Reeva viewed it as a stepping stone.

Her portfolio contained a huge variety of styles and poses. She loved the play-acting side of modelling; she could take on a range of roles – from a tough-glam girl member of a SWAT team for a cinema commercial for Pin Pop lollipops to the yummy mummy cover girl for Afrikaans parenting magazine *Baba & Kleuter*. She flew between Johannesburg and Cape Town for the cities' respective annual fashion weeks in October and July, and to film and shoot some of the leading national campaigns for brands such as Toyota, Clover and the Italian designer label Zui. When you get your *FHM* cover, they produce a book bound to the main magazine to present the new cover girl. In *Introducing Reeva*, she posed in roles based on a Marilyn Monroe theme. She could play lots of different parts and project different attitudes. I loved her modelling – because, as her mother, I loved bragging about it. She'd phone up and say, 'Mummy, get this magazine and that magazine.' I had to. I made it compulsory for her to tell me whenever she was in a publication, and then I'd go and get the magazine and show it to, well, anyone and everyone! She could be in a military-style autumn/winter fashion spread or a 'new nudes' summer special; she looked beautiful in full-on red-carpet glamour for Pallu, the exclusive designer clothing shop, and very sophisticated for Zui, an Italian emporium. It's horrible really, bragging that way, but I was so proud of her. That's how I felt. Your kids are your pride and joy, aren't they? You gave birth to them.

Barry's attitude towards her modelling did not become more enthusiastic. Of course he was proud of her and the effort she put in, but he didn't like the *FHM* shoots. He'd say, yes, they're beautiful pictures, but she hasn't got enough clothes on. He was worried that the more visible she became, the more she'd be at risk of being followed home or attacked after leaving an event. He just didn't like her being so far away in Johannesburg.

Through sheer hard work, her profile grew year by year in the seven years she spent modelling professionally from 2006 to 2013. As *FHM* editor Hagen Engler commented after she was killed, she was just so obsessed with making something out of herself and prepared to do what she needed to get there. Even though she was such a friendly, lovely person, she was ruthlessly dedicated to that part of being a model. She would do a hundred press-ups, a hundred sit-ups, lunges, squats, the stretches, the weights. I mean, her body was superb when she got her *FHM* break, but she had to toil away in the gym to get that. She had to go back to be appraised and re-appraised three times. Twice Hagen sent her away and said she needed to hone her physique harder. That is the sort of dedication she went to Johannesburg prepared to commit to – and it wasn't easy, not least because she worried that she was wasting her hard-earned degree status.

Work meant work on many levels – maintaining her body and appearance in the gym and salon, attending industry events, attending auditions, then participating in the shoots either in studios or locations. The rhythms of the modelling season structured her life in Johannesburg and with it came a social life in terms of launches, industry fairs, fashion shows and red-carpet fixtures, and access to a widening circle of friends involved in the business. I'd go to stay with her and get a glimpse of how she spent her downtime. It was fun – pizza and drinks with friends, chilling in front of movies because work could be so intense, baking for the girls at the agency and lounging at home with her cats.

She caught up with her fellow law student friend Kristin when she, too, came to the big city to work for Standard Bank about a year later. Kristin gathered that Reeva had been exposed to some bad experiences in her settling-in period when she first moved to Johannesburg, but that she soon found her own life. Early on Reeva spoke about how guilty she felt at times that she wasn't doing something with her degree, but Kristin told her not to think like that, reminding her that modelling meant she could pay her bills and have the freedom to pick and choose jobs, and that she could return to law later. At some stage she did speak to advocates about taking up a pupillage. She went for some interviews, but it never panned out. The problem is you earn very little money when you take up a pupillage, and it's a full-time training. It would be impossible to support herself without a job and impossible to combine with modelling.

Modelling demands a mindset and a physical set of requirements beyond most nine-to-five jobs. Abigail and Reeva were both back in Port Elizabeth for Christmas early in their five-year plan. On one level, Reeva had grown comfortable as the polished, urban-based model, but at heart she loved reverting to relaxed country girl at home with us. The girls spent a lot of time together wearing old clothes and going around in bare feet. Reeva loved Abigail's family farm – they have a pool and horses and lots of animals. One night she slept over and the next day Reeva was up bright and early in a pair of luminous Crocs, helping to muck out the stables, pushing the wheelbarrow while Abigail shovelled up the horse poo.

Abigail was shocked by how very, very skinny Reeva had become to fit in with the modelling ideal. So, too, was her old maths teacher who bumped into her in the Walmer shopping mall. As her mother, I preferred to see her in her more natural voluptuous shape too, but it was an indication of how disciplined life as a model had to be. 'Our relationship was always that I was the dead frank honest one. There was no making it pretty with me,' Abigail tells me. 'Reeva, on the other hand, was the one who loved everybody and could be a bit airy-fairy. I remember saying to her, "*What* has happened to you?" And she was like, "Yeah, well, it's very hard, it's very competitive, there's a lot of cattiness." Snacking on Nachos that my mom had made and drinking bottles of absolutely magnificent pink JC Leroux and fruit juice, we spent hours talking about how she was coping, how she was going to continue to cope, and I remember saying to her again, "Just make sure you don't lose yourself in that place. Always remember the barefoot Reeva.'"

As we saw at her funeral, the reality was that Reeva lived two lives. She lived a PE life and she lived a Johannesburg life, and those two lives did not mix. Those friends did not mix. She kept her work life separate from her home life. She could do that because she didn't differentiate between people herself; she had an innate way of fitting in and she had a natural way of stopping to count her blessings whatever situation she found herself in. As Abigail put it, it didn't matter if you were a homeless person or Miss Hoity Toity, it didn't matter what walk of life you came from, Reeva always had the time of day for everyone – and that was her gift. But thinking of others before herself meant she took on everyone's problems and rarely complained herself. She used to say that she was working to look after us in our old age. For a girl who craved family life, and adored her extended family, the move to Johannesburg gave her some inner turmoil. She didn't like being separated from her family but at the same time she knew it was her best chance at earning a good living and establishing the profile which would later allow her to practise her ambitions in law.

The good news was that soon after Reeva arrived in Johannesburg she met a wonderful man, Warren Lahoud, a perfect gentleman who treated her like a queen. He was such a good person, ambitious, hard working, going forward in life, and he treated her so well. He was so thoughtful. On her birthday he would scatter a trail of rose petals from the door to the bed, and buy her piles of presents. He would choose clothes in shops for her and put them on the side so she could go back and try them on and be absolutely sure she really loved them. He bought her Jimmy Choo shoes, and a dishwasher because he didn't want her doing dishes. He whisked her to New York and the first thing they did when they got off the plane was to find a legendary Starbucks in New York City and have a coffee. (There are no Starbucks outlets in South Africa.) Warren was like someone sent from heaven in man terms.

When they first met, Reeva contacted Abigail in London to tell her about him. As usual, the girls just picked up where they left off. They were very different in many ways, but they just fitted arm in arm even when they lived in different hemispheres. Abigail remembers a long message exchange via their computers one weekend in which Reeva said she'd met the most amazing guy. 'Go and have a little stalk!' she told Abigail.

'She gives me his name and the first thing I see is that he's younger than her,' Abigail tells me. 'Before I'd gone to London and she'd gone to Johannesburg, I'd told her to go to Johannesburg and find herself a nice man, not a boy. When I saw Warren's age I messaged back asking why she had fallen for this boy? He was a few years younger than her. "You know what's going to happen," I typed. "You're going to grow older and you're going to outgrow each other. You're going to break your heart and you're going to be a mess." She was like, "Oh, Abi, you're always so sensible, how can you be such a dampener?" And I was saying, "I'm not being a dampener, I'm telling you how it's most likely going to be."'

Reeva and Warren were very happy and lived together for five or six years. She brought him home and Barry loved him. He could see he would look after her. Abigail met him, too, when she was flying out to London. Reeva spent the afternoon with her in Johannesburg airport while she waited to get the connecting flight to Heathrow and she brought Warren along. Abigail said she could see he was lovely and that they were great around each other. She could tell by the way he spoke to her that he treated her with respect.

For a long time Reeva and Warren lived happily with their two cats, Milk and Panther. They ran a fruit and vegetable company together that exported fresh produce to Saudi Arabia and Mauritius, and installed fresh produce inside Makro stores throughout South Africa. Reeva realised that modelling income could be good, but erratic, so she made sure she had income from other sources. Often, they'd be up at 3 a.m. going to the market, then they might both go to the gym together, and on to the office which was in Warren's mother's home. They worked hard and they enjoyed a fun social life, meeting up with friends in the evening, going to the cinema, enjoying the young buzz of the big city. Warren was away travelling a lot, but he loved coming home, because Reeva was a homemaker. 'She made everything warm,' he told me. 'I'd walk in and everything was nice and warm.' Reeva had lots of new friends from the modelling industry, but liked to stay close to her old PE friends, such as Kristin, who were so important to her. She once left a message for Kim and something in her intonation made Kim realise she was feeling a bit down. She called her straight away and said, 'Coz, are you okay?' Reeva said she was fed up with the fake people in Johannesburg, she missed her real friends.

Initially Kristin and Reeva lived in neighbouring complexes, but when Reeva moved to Warren's house on the other side of town the two girls made sure they met up regularly. At least once a month they'd go and have tea and cake together for a one-to-one chat. There's a chain in South Africa called Exclusive Books and the girls' favourite thing to do was to go for what they called their Exclusive session – sharing their news and feelings about life with each other. Now Reeva's gone, I love hearing from her friends about the fun and camaraderie they used to take for granted. 'Typically we'd grab a pile of magazines and laugh and talk about boys,' Kristin told me. 'She'd have her favourite Red Cappuccino made from Rooibos tea and we both valued that time.' Because Kristin is a bank worker, in Compliance, she had a good perspective on Reeva's world, and vice versa. The girls in the modelling industry are tough on themselves and tough on each other. Other girls could be so bitchy that Reeva wouldn't be praised on her achievements. From Kristin's perspective in banking, she'd tell her what an amazing achievement things like her *FHM* cover was. She'd say to her, 'You're only young once. You can look back one day and say, "Oh my word, I had such a good body!" Go for it.' She supported it. Reeva did have some misgivings, she was conscious of the lads' mag image, but Kristin would reassure her that it wasn't as if she were posing nude!

And Reeva would compliment Kristin. 'She didn't hold everyone up to the crazy expectations of her industry,' she told me. 'She could see beauty in average people. She was a really, really good friend.' The girls loved going to the Jewish area of Johannesburg. They often talked about getting a mezuzah – a scroll inscribed with Hebrew verses that is traditionally fixed to the door of Jewish homes. They loved to visit a particular store in the Jewish shopping centre to get things for baking. They both loved to bake and eat cake. Kristin says Reeva was always up for going out to have cake together. On rare occasions, if she had a big job coming up, she'd say she couldn't, but she wasn't uptight about eating. One time Kristin called her after she'd had a minor car accident, just a fender bender, to tell her what happened and say she was going to get checked out at the hospital. Reeva insisted on coming to sit with her in the waiting room. 'I told her that it wasn't necessary, but she came anyway and sat with me for several hours. That's the kind of friend she was,' she says. 'Another time, I was moving flats within a complex and she literally turned up and helped me move all my belongings, bag by bag.'

Kristin and Reeva never spoke about returning to Port Elizabeth. She thinks it may have initially been her plan to move back one day, but she had found her own life in Johannesburg with Warren. If anywhere, she thinks she would have eventually moved to Cape Town: 'We'd say ideally we wouldn't want to raise children in Johannesburg.'

Reeva loved Cape Town. It was where her beloved

grandpa lived and home to her cousin Kim, her childhood comrade, to whom she had grown close again as a grown woman. Twice, Reeva stayed for prolonged periods with Kim. She travelled there for a month, first, in 2011 to see if there was a market for her in the Cape modelling scene. She was accompanying Warren, who was opening up a branch of his Freshmart produce stores inside the Makro store in Montague Gardens, and they were due to stay in a guest house with Warren's appointed branch manager and assistant. Reeva, however, was quickly on the phone to ask if she could come and stay with Kim because the guest-house shower was dirty and the room smelled. Kim's son Jason had moved out to stay with his girlfriend so they had an extra room and Reeva ended up staying a month. She craved the warmth and bustle of family life. She'd ask Kim what was for supper each night so that she could help shop and cook and make it a special occasion. She'd asked when they were going to visit Lyn – Kim's mum, her aunt – and then sug-gest they go over that afternoon. She'd enquire how often Kim saw her sister Sharon and work out a plan. Kim says she gave off irresistible energy. Dion, Kim's husband, loved it when Reeva was in the house because all he heard was laughing. There was such happiness in the house. She joked, she baked, she gave so much. She had an amazing influence on the whole family.

Reeva next came back for six months, flying to and from Johannesburg, dipping her toe in the modelling market in Cape Town and again helping Warren out. 'She was like an angel in everything she gifted us,' says Kim, who is so grateful to the difference Reeva made to her teenagers' lives. Reeva loved catching up with Kim and Dion, but she sensed the children needed her more, so she made a point of connecting with Gypsy and Rain. She took bonding with them very seriously. She would sit by the pool and tan with them, spend quality time chatting about the ups and downs they were experiencing as teenagers, making popcorn, watching films, giving them advice, just laughing and giggling. She'd write 'I love my family [insert smiley face]' on the kitchen board and put up different inspirational quotes each day. Dion and Kim would go out to dinner and when they came home late they'd be careful not to wake up Reeva. She had become the mother of their house too! When she came in from work, she'd walk in and call out 'Helloooo?' And this became a thing after she went back to Johannesburg. Everyone would walk in and say 'Hellooooo?'

Reeva had a particularly special bond with Gypsy, who was having a troubled time as a teenager. She did so much for her, largely by making it clear that she was always there for her. One day Gypsy was due to do a five-kilometre walk with her school and she insisted Reeva accompany her, so this twenty-eight-year-old woman climbed in the van and went to school for the day. Gypsy's whole grade were in awe of this beautiful, friendly model and that, in turn, made Gypsy feel special. That was typical Reeva. She was so right-eous, so ready to help other people. She was there to take on everything for everyone. Family was more important to her than anything else.

As much as we had misgivings about her being in Johannesburg, she seemed very sorted and structured about her life there. Whenever she came home to visit us, especially for Christmas, we knew what to expect. She'd go straight to check the fridge, which was never clean. One year she fired the girl who worked in the house because she didn't clean between the tiles on the floor. She liked everything to be clean and in order. She was a neat freak before she even went to Johannesburg. She'd get irritated by me and Barry in our senile state, you know. I used to say, 'One day you'll realise ...' but she'd say, 'No, I'll never be like that.' When she travelled back to Johannesburg, she left a long list of chores that Barry had to do and I had to do on a daily basis. That's how she was. Her wardrobe, her drawers, everything was immaculately tidy. That's why when I saw her jeans lying on the floor in Oscar's bedroom – that fact came up in the trial – her friends and I all knew they'd been moved for sure: because she would *never* leave them on the floor. She was tidy to the extreme, OCD big time. There was something wrong about those clothes allegedly found strewn on the floor. Her friends said the same. She was always impeccably tidy. I keep trying to find sense in what happened that night and I think she tried to be like that for him, polished and perfect in her own way, and I think she just irritated him. Because he liked to be the one in control and she wouldn't like to be told what to do or how to be.

She had her own pride and her own dignity about how she carried herself. This extended to me. She didn't like me having a drink when she was younger. She'd say to me, 'Mommy, we're going home now. You're not looking good.' She didn't drink much at all herself. She liked to be in control. I would have liked her sometimes not to be that controlled. For me, a glass of wine is a relaxation. You don't have to be drunk. It's just about chatting and talking rubbish and switching off after a hard day's work.

Three Months With Oscar

Christmas 2012 was the first Reeva did not spend with us in twenty-nine years. In October, she sent us a message to say she wanted to treat the two of us to a weekend with her in Kuzuku Lodge in the Addo Elephant National Park, an amazing conservation reserve for elephants, buffalo and black rhino with beautiful colonies of gannets and penguins. It's a special place, but I realised immediately that this was to prepare us for her not coming home for Christmas because she had never missed one year ever. She asked me to break the news gently to Barry. As it turned out, she gave us a wonderful time in Addo – game drives, lovely dinner parties in the evening, just the three of us. Perfect.

She had split up with Warren after five or six years and had been seeing Francois Hougaard, the Springbok rugby union player, and he was phoning her often during the weekend. They were close but Reeva said she had decided they should just be friends. She genuinely liked him, I know, but having recently come out of a long-term relationship she didn't want to jump into anything too quickly and she didn't want to be part of a celebrity stable. She was twenty-nine and she wanted someone to settle down with in good time. She was looking for a soul mate and Francois was five years younger. Another boy! She'd never discussed with me about wanting to have babies, but I believe she was starting to think that way. We all get to that stage. When I asked about him, she said, 'Mama, Francois is very style-conscious. He puts a lot of thought into the way he dresses. He has about twenty different watches and matches his shoes very carefully . . . ' And she didn't want that kind of person. Lots of girls run after those kind of guys, but Reeva was at heart a simple, home-loving kind of girl. She didn't want to run with a pack. And once she'd made up her mind, that would be that. Girls who are pretty learn early on not to tolerate nonsense because they often attract the wrong kind of guy. When *FHM* asked her to name her favourite spot on Earth for their 'Introducing Reeva' feature, she'd replied: 'On a hammock in my grandpa's back garden in Cape Town. I can't go there any more because he's no longer with us, but I dream about that place every day.' The red-carpet life came with her work as a model; it was not what she wanted in the long term.

Oscar had seen Reeva somewhere and asked a mutual friend to introduce them. They met over lunch on 4 November 2012, through Justin Divaris, the chief executive officer of Daytona Group which distributes McLaren cars, at a racing event at the Kyalami grand prix circuit in Gauteng. At this event Reeva laughingly agreed to accompany Oscar that evening to the South African Sports Awards 2012 because he did not have a date. It was a spur-of-the-moment thing for her, although it turned out he had long set his eyes on her. A friend rang the next day and pointed me towards coverage of the event on YouTube. I looked it up and saw her on the red carpet as his guest at the ceremony, which was held at the Sandton Convention Centre. They looked very sparky, very amused to be in each other's company at such short notice. She was wearing an elegant pale pink halter-neck fringed dress with her long blonde hair held back in a simple chic ponytail. I was thinking, who is this man? I called to ask her if this was a new special friend. She said no, she'd just accepted his invitation as a friend. The day after the event, she really didn't seem to appreciate the public specu-lation that came from them being seen together.

It may sound strange, when he was hailed by the world as the Blade Runner, but I don't follow sport, I'm not a great

143

reader of newspapers, and I'd never heard of Oscar Pistorius. Reeva had never mentioned him before. I honestly didn't know who Oscar Pistorius was. I've always liked the name Oscar. It's a beautiful name; it has presence. I've since learnt that most people knew and admired him because, as South Africans, they were so proud of him for his charitable achievements in helping victims of landmines and other children who had lost their legs, and for all the wonderful barriers he had broken through as a Paralympian sprinter. But I wasn't aware of him as a personality, a role model and athletic superstar, none of that – and I wasn't used to seeing my daughter on the arm of a man other than Warren Lahoud.

To our mind, Warren was the perfect gentleman for our daughter. When she brought him home to meet us, we all clicked. Barry and I could see he treated her with tremendous love and respect, but by the early autumn of 2012 she had broken up with him. I don't really know why. They seemed so happy and well suited for so long. As the years went by, though, Warren never asked *that* question. Reeva didn't say anything to me on the subject of a proposal because she loved him and she wouldn't want me to feel ill of him, but I imagine she thought if he hadn't asked her to marry him after five or six years, when she was approaching thirty, then maybe he never would. There comes a time when you think, is it ever going to happen? I think she was secretly hoping for a surprise engagement. Maybe she decided she couldn't continue with him for another five years in case he never intended to marry her. Maybe she wanted children and he wasn't ready. I do know that she adored Warren, but she'd started to ask herself serious questions – you know, I'm nearly thirty, can we move forward with this? Can we have kids? She thought about the future very carefully. She was evolving as a woman and starting to ask herself different questions about what she wanted from life.

Friends like Kristin could not understand why she wanted to split up with him either. She said she still found him attractive. She could see he was a provider. She insisted whoever he married would be a very lucky woman. They remained on friendly terms but initially she was in two minds about that; she wanted Warren to move on with his life. 'As a friend who was always single, who knew how terrible it is on the dating scene, I couldn't understand it,' Kristin says. 'I thought she'd get her fingers burnt – not in the way she did, obviously – but she'd see what it was like out there and come back to Warren. They were so good together.'

The truth is her career was taking off. After all her hard work, her extremely professional approach to looking after herself and to interpreting briefs for casting sessions, she was becoming truly high profile. Always modest, she did privately acknowledge that she was in a position now when people recognised her in public places whereas, before, she could walk around totally unnoticed. She was conscious of being on the radar and that was fulfilling in that it was a sign she had become successful. Having been a late starter, she had grafted away and evolved into the calibre of model who could feature in the *FHM* Calendar 2011 (as the October girl) and a sexy shoot for *FHM* Collections. The *FHM* association was solid. She was voted #40 out of their list of the hundred most beautiful women in the world in 2011 and #45 in 2012; and the prized feature of her portfolio was the cover-girl shoot for the prized December issue in 2011. Oh my word, she worked hard for it. She went back to be seen by editor Hagen Engler three times. Twice he said, no, you're still a bit overweight, and she'd go away, consult a nutritionist, hit the gym, do her routine of skipping, lunges, a hundred press-ups and a hundred sit-ups a day. The third time she went back he said he nearly fell off the chair and he gave her the December cover.

So, what with all the buzz leading up to filming *Tropika* as well, she was out on the radar of the glamorous Johannesburg scene, invited as a fixture to all sorts of events, posing for photographers for the social columns. Maintaining a glamorous profile is a vital part of being a sought-after model — and Warren wasn't part of that world. He was a workaholic in his own sphere. To run their fruit and vegetable export business, he was often up in the small hours to go to the wholesalers market and often out of the country. He wasn't part of Reeva's modelling world with its increasing late-night, bright-light demands. When they were together in Johannesburg they shared the same work ethic: both very disciplined about going to the gym before heading off to work. But socially they were moving in opposite directions, operating in different time zones.

When she told us she was going to break up with Warren, we couldn't understand it. And then she ends up with this gun-toting guy. Barry was particularly upset because he loved Warren. Although he thought Johannesburg was a more dangerous place for Reeva than Port Elizabeth, he felt she was safe with Warren because he absolutely worshipped her. It was hard for her, moving to a competitive, brittle city like Johannesburg, and she was lucky to find stability and security early on in her domestic life with Warren. She used to buy me a plane ticket and I'd go to stay with her for a week. We did that often. It was great fun, catching up, chatting. I loved going to stay there. She had decorated their flat in a lovely, modern way with a huge outsize clock on the wall and a brown leather lounge suite. The cats' sleeping box took pride of place and their toys were neatly stored around the room. She had everything ordered just so. Kim remembers once when Reeva was staying with her in Cape Town, Warren called asking where something might be, and Reeva replied, telling him precisely that it was five centimetres from something on the second shelf of a particular cupboard. She had everyone organised. Her Johannesburg friends were different, hi-faluting people, but she included me in everything she did. We'd go out with a group to a restaurant or whatever and she'd tell her friends they'd have to put up with me as well! I've still got one of those letters she sent inviting me for a visit. '*I really don't want to enclose too much info now cos I want to save everything for when I see you. YAY. We're going to drink wine, drink coffee, watch movies and chat, chat, chat!!!*' She was so generous in sharing her life.

After the split, she moved out of the house she shared with Warren and rented a room in a friend's house as a short-term measure. She stayed there for seven months but she'd phoned her father to say she wanted to move on and get her own place, it wasn't working out. Barry became very worked up and fretful about Reeva's safety now she was lodging; he kept begging her to come home. By Christmas he had an overwhelming need to have her back with us in Port Elizabeth. He'd imagine her being tailed home after one of these red-carpet events full of gorgeous people wearing expensive watches and jewellery. It could be that a lot of it is urban myth, but you always hear stories of how dangerous Johannesburg can be, especially for a young woman. We'd hear of muggings and car-jackings and horrible incidents occurring at knife or gunpoint. Barry would ring and plead with her to move back. It was like he had a sixth sense that something bad was going to happen to her.

In the autumn of 2012, Reeva was going through a lot emotionally because she wasn't a person who could be unkind. When she suggested they go their separate ways, Warren was devastated and she couldn't stand that she was causing him pain. She carried a lot of guilt because she didn't want to break his heart. It's like a divorce, she said to Kim. I do feel sympathy for Warren because he said that in his head he just assumed they were going to be together for the rest of their lives. He wanted to buy a house for her and give her all sorts of things. Maybe if he had communicated that to her, things would have turned out differently. But life was taking them in opposing directions. They hardly saw each other. So they split in late August. She met and became close to Francois Hougaard in September/October before they decided to keep things platonic, and then on 4 November she met Oscar through this Justin Divaris guy, who was also a friend of Francois's.

By his own account, Oscar was persistent in his pursuit of her. In court he described himself as 'besotted' and told his lawyer Barry Roux, 'I was very keen on Reeva. If anything,

I was more keen than she was.' He insisted on seeing her every day for the first seven days after their initial date at the Sports Awards. Those close to her suggested she felt 'caged in' and 'stalked'. Her landlord in Johannesburg, Cecil Myers, Gina's father, felt obliged to warn him to 'back off' as Oscar forced himself on her emotionally. He said he found him superficially polite, but very moody, hasty and impatient. Other friends said she found him overwhelming. On 30 November, at the British Olympic Ball in the Grosvenor House Hotel in London, a glowing Oscar showed people on his table at dinner a picture stored on his phone of 'this amazing girl' – Reeva – saying she was going to be the perfect girlfriend for him. Beyond her vivaciousness and her beauty, he said he liked the fact that she was a bit older than him, mature and dedicated to her career.

Oscar's persistence paid off. How, or why, she decided to be with him is something I keep trying to work out. I once met a man who said he had special powers and he informed me one of my daughters was a powerful personality with a strong will – and that would be Reeva, I thought – and my other daughter would always be in trouble because she believes everything people say to her, especially men. Well, Simone has a lovely, wonderful heart and she can't say 'no'; in fact, she can't spell 'no'. This man hadn't met either of them, but that was how I thought of them in my mind.

Simone has been married three times, and though I did fear that Reeva also wore her heart on her sleeve I thought she was so *aware*. And look at what happened to her. I think ultimately she felt sorry for Oscar. She would have seen him as vulnerable and she probably thought she could make things better for him. She was a nurturer, a carer, she wanted to look after him. And as Abigail says, Reeva was a rainbow and fairies kind of person, always seeing the pretty side of things and thinking the best of people. She admired his achievements as a double amputee. She found his intensity attractive. They kept whatever was going on between them, or not going on yet, quiet and private. In the middle of November her Twitter feed – a very public forum – suggests underlying turmoil among all her happy posts highlighting industry events, launches and product recommendations:

They said Reeva baby use your head. But I chose to use my heart instead.

By the end of November she had started acknowledging a friendship with Oscar, retweeting his philosophical nuggets:

'The world breaks everyone, and afterward, some are strong at the broken places.' Wise words for an amazing person @OscarPistorius.

A post on 3 December read –

I'm so disappointed in myself today, more than anyone else. I never learn from the past. How do you grow if you never learn? #sadheart.

On 6 December she is playful again:

Wondering what my stalker is up to? Kinda miss him lurking around tonight . . .

By the middle of December, she was again retweeting a sentiment from **Oscar: Everything happens for a reason. Practice some faith in yourself and others. Pray and trust that His will shall prevail . . .** Soon afterwards she posted her own sentiment: **Love comes from finding someone who makes you feel comfortable with yourself. Almost like finding the other part of yourself.**

Clearly she was re-assessing what she expected or wanted from love and romance and a relationship. Theirs was not a consciously public romance in November and December 2012, but they started being seen together at the same events. Reeva told me he was a very, very good man. She was impressed by his charity work and his fundraising projects for children who had lost legs. They shared a love of fast cars, of horse racing and animals. Oscar had two dogs and owned racehorses. On a superficial level, they made a beautiful couple, thrilling gossip columnists with the ultimate high-profile celebrity match of sporting hero and dazzling model. But after one early red–carpet appearance together her publicist, Sarit Thompson, rang me and said, 'June, I'm very worried. He's so *possessive.*' They'd been at an event the night before and he was keeping her away from people. People at the event wanted to talk to her, not him, and he got annoyed about that. Sarit was worried that he had an unnatural obsession for her. He pursued her intently. I gently asked Reeva about this aspect of his personality and she said that on one occasion very, very early in their friendship he had cried and cried because she wouldn't go out with him. After that, she wasn't keen on disclosing things about him that she knew I'd worry about or warn her off.

One of the things that would have bonded Reeva and Oscar strongly was their mutual attraction to speed and performance cars. There was another resident on the Silver Woods Country Estate in the east of Pretoria where Oscar had his home, a man called Michael Nhlengethwa who'd done very well and who shared a fascination with sports cars with his neighbour. One day they were admiring a stunning new vehicle when Oscar said he wanted Michael to meet Reeva. He called her out and actually introduced her to him as his 'fiancée' – no one had ever heard him say this before. The man put out his hand to shake hers, but she had her arms out to hug him. That was her open heart. And he was overwhelmed.

Another day Reeva called me from a car. She said, 'Mama, I'm scared. I'm in the car with Oscar and he's driving like a lunatic at 260 kilometres an hour.' I asked her to put the phone to his ear and I said to him, 'Listen, if you hurt my baby, I will have you wiped out', or words to that effect. I didn't mean that as a threat, I was trying to keep to the spirit of fun they were obviously having – Darren Fresco, a friend of Reeva's, was also in the car – but I wanted to make it very clear that he had a responsibility to look after my daughter. I couldn't bear to think her life was in danger at his hands. He said, 'Yes, Mrs Steenkamp,' and Reeva said he slowed down straight away.

That was the only time I ever spoke to him – and it was to issue a warning.

Ironically, her friend Darren had taken her ex, Warren, car shopping one day and Oscar was there too. Kristin tells me it was the three of them together. What a bizarre combination. Apparently Warren quietly told Oscar that he must promise to look after Reeva.

I was a bit worried about the new 'fast life' she might be living after the speeding experience, but I can't say I sensed any danger signals. Having split from Warren, she was foot-loose and fancy free, as they say. I did not know these people she was hanging out with or that they went around Johannesburg with guns, firing out of the car roof, handling firearms in family restaurants, going to shooting ranges for a laugh. I knew nothing about how he was an adrenalin junkie who liked all this macho stuff and had more guns on order to bring his firearm collection up to ten. I still had my weekly long chatty phone call with Reeva every Saturday but she didn't volunteer much about him. We were very close, but you are private about some things with your mother, aren't you? If I'd known, I'd have said, 'Listen, I don't think this is going to work'. Not that she would listen! She never mentioned him to Barry, or to Abigail, and that is a sure sign that she wasn't convinced the relationship would develop or stay the course. She wouldn't announce a boyfriend to Barry or Abigail unless it were for real.

I look back now and see that that was the beginning of us losing touch somehow over the three months when she was seeing him. It torments me that I didn't pick up on the clues that suggest she was struggling. I regret not noticing the warning signs that all was not well in her life and questioning her further. But she was twenty-nine and I wanted to respect the fact that she had chosen to split with Warren and take her life in a different direction. I can see now she was adjusting to so many changes: a change of relationship, a change of home, an approaching milestone thirtieth birthday and a blank page in terms of her plans for the future. She was asking herself a lot of questions. She was hiding her uncertainty, I think, and maybe her suffering. She wouldn't want me to know that she was having a difficult time, because if she hurt, I hurt.

I do know that she was particularly upset to hear that after she moved out of Warren's house, her beloved black and white cats Panther and Milk had disappeared. They were wild cats who had appeared in their garden. She had fed them and when it was clear they regarded her as their owner, she had had their ears clipped and had them neutered, as the law requires you to do with wild cats. She adored them and they ran away the day she left Warren's house, perhaps to find her. It really hit a nerve with her, that her decision to move out had such a negative impact on her cats. She felt guilty and distraught. She was a big animal lover. Initially she was going to send both cats to me, but changed her mind because she thought I had enough worries and Powder would probably have eaten them anyway. She asked the guy who took over their place to leave food and drink out, but Panther was never seen again. Reeva was heartbroken. Milk returned, and she sent him on his own to Kim. He moved on to Kim's sister, Sharon, and then disappeared again. The funny thing is he was eventually found alive and well, staying with another family close by who have adopted him.

Reeva was very disorientated that winter of 2012/13. She became a bit depressed, I think. Whenever she suffered emotionally, she fell ill. I get the feeling she was evaluating her life, asking herself questions about what she wanted as a woman. She was very wrapped up in trying to puzzle out the potential of a relationship with Oscar and considering whether it had a future. Their relationship seemed very stop and start. When it was going well, they had fun together. She called him a sexy boy and found him beautiful to look at. She thought him smart and classy, and they had common ground in needing to eat well and look after their bodies for their careers. He had an intensity she was drawn to, but the flip-side of that was that she told me they were fighting a lot, always initiated by him, often – to her embarrassment – in public. At some stage, at some function, she and Oscar had a fight in the car park. Several people told me it had been commented on in the papers and magazines.

In one phone call, when I asked how it was going, she said, 'Mommy, we're arguing all the time.' I said, 'But what can you be fighting about in such a new relationship?' And she said, 'Mommy, you can't understand what it's about.' When their WhatsApp exchanges were revealed in court, everyone could see the controlling and demoralising nit-picking he imposed on her: Don't do this. Don't do that. Don't chew gum. Don't speak like that. (I think she'd had some part on TV and she had to speak in an American accent, and maybe she was practising and it annoyed him.) You can't wear this. You must wear that. It was heartbreaking to hear how she had tried to make him proud of her when they went to an event and her dismay when he'd publicly cause a scene and walk off in a huff. She was tiptoeing around this man's moods – and that was not like Reeva. She told me on the phone how they were at one event and he said huffily that he had to eat at a particular time, something to do with his special diet regime, and abruptly announced he was leaving immediately. She had very high shoes on and didn't want to hold him up, so she let him walk out while she followed as fast as she could to the exit, but he drove off without her. When they discussed it later, he accused her instead of chatting up some guy and ignoring him. That was why he'd turned on his heels, nothing to do with an eating regime. She was very upset to be treated like that.

Kristin says everything Reeva mentioned about Oscar gave her misgivings. She understood he had a nasty temper, but thought the problems were more that everything to do with him was a huge drama. From what she said, he'd flip about a lot of things. Reeva had a role in an advert and part of the script involved her kissing a man. She was very nervous about telling Oscar. Her friends kept asking, 'Have you told him yet?' And she hadn't. She couldn't face it. And she was embarrassed to admit it, because it was so out of character. She was too scared of how he would respond. He was so possessive. When Kristin was out with Reeva once, she pointed out how ridiculous Oscar looked dressed up in a red silk jacket on the cover of GQ *Style* spring/summer magazine 2012/13. Reeva said, 'Don't ever say that to him!' As if Kristin would. She's not a rude person and Reeva knew that better than anyone, but it shows how she was always anticipating an angry reaction from him. Another time, she'd told Kristin how his bull terrier had killed a dachshund, which upset her very much as an animal lover (and a dachsy owner herself), but again Reeva begged Kristin never to mention this around him. There were so many things she shouldn't say or do around him and Kristin thought, *why* is she pussyfooting around this guy? It was so unlike her.

I think the difficulties stemmed from him being accustomed to calling the shots about everything in his life. As an athlete, he was surrounded by an entourage. As a role model in South Africa, he was used to being cosseted and treated as the guy at the top. He wanted her to be Oscar's Girlfriend. But she wouldn't want that. She was Reeva. She was completely feminine, but she had a mind of her own. Although she was nervous of his reaction to things, she would not have always been able to quash her assertive self – and some men don't like that. It was up and down on that front. Reeva used to go into the offices of ICE Models once a week to take in banana bread she'd baked for all the girls. Twice, she brought Oscar into the agency, and according to Jane he was happy to take a back seat. He knew this was her place, her home, she told me. All the girls at the agency dropped in regularly for coffee and a chat. They had boys in there, and mums and sisters. They were all very close. They all shared what was going on in their lives. 'With Oscar, it was such a new relationship we only saw him twice,' Jane said. 'He was one of those men who phone seventeen times a day. He was like that in November and early December and it was too much for Reeva. They had a break over December. She gave him a second chance in the New Year and then they became quite serious quite quickly.'

I wonder now, if it had been a man who was not a lauded celebrity, whether there might have been more of a red flag for Reeva? How much of an unattractive attitude did she dismiss because he was a golden boy, an ambassador for the Paralympian movement, who achieved his fame surrounded by a tight-knit close circle? How much was she flattered to have won his heart? Perhaps her empathy towards all he had overcome in life blinded her judgement? In falling for Oscar, she accepted the whole package. If only we'd known what was going on, but we respected her desire to spend the festive season independently from us that year.

Barry was unhappy about Reeva's relationship with Oscar. She hadn't officially announced it to him, but I'd briefed him of course. He couldn't clarify exactly what his misgivings were. She and Oscar were supposed to spend Christmas and New Year together. From what I can gather, he decided instead to go to a bachelor party in Cape Town. She ended up spending Christmas Day with Kristin, and then he came to fetch her from Kristin's mother's house later that day, and I know she ended up on her own again on New Year's Eve. I was more than a thousand kilometres away and have been grateful to Kristin for telling me how it played out.

Kristin said it was just her and Reeva and a few other friends around as a lot of people don't stay in Johannesburg for Xmas, they head to the coast. Oscar had gone to Cape Town just before Christmas without including her and he had asked her to look after his house for him. She invited Kristin to come and stay with her there in Pretoria because she was very uncomfortable being alone in his big empty luxury house. Kristin's car was giving her problems and she didn't want to risk driving the fifty kilometres. Reeva said she'd come and fetch her, and promised to take her to and from work in her car. That's the kind of friend she was. Kristin said she thought it was so weird that Oscar left her alone to look after his house. He was happy to do that – and over Christmas. Reeva messaged Kristin to say she had nowhere to go at Christmas. Kristin was going to her aunt's house and checked that it was okay for Reeva to come too. Kristin said she could not bring herself to ask Reeva why she wasn't spending Christmas with Oscar or whether he'd got her anything for Christmas. It remained an unspoken thing between them. She found the whole situation awkward.

Reeva arrived at Kristin's on 25 December in Oscar's white BMW and they had Christmas lunch. Her aunt had cooked a Springbok pie and Reeva ate everything! I gather she spoke a lot about him that day. It was Oscar this and Oscar that. Kristin's granny had no idea who she was talking about. Reeva didn't put him in a context. It was so unlike her. Kristin felt Reeva was not in love with him, but seemed a bit star-struck.

At 3 p.m. Oscar arrived in his Audi to fetch Reeva and his BMW. Kristin's brother and cousin went outside to say hello and Reeva came inside and said she was so cross with Oscar because he was swearing at his friend and she didn't like him swearing in front of Kristin's family. Kristin herself didn't have the desire to go out to meet him. 'I assumed this whole Oscar episode was a short-lived thing,' she told me. 'They weren't on a romantic footing as a couple; she hadn't slept with him. She was nervous about that. Oscar came inside and said to me,

"I've heard so much about you," and I had to bite my tongue. I wanted to say, "I haven't heard anything about you. You're not that special!" My entire family was in the lounge, including my granny, who didn't have her hearing aid in properly. He introduced himself as Oscar and Granny shouted back, "Sorry. Who are you?" That was funny, but I did appreciate that he sat and chatted a bit before he left with Reeva.'

Again, he wasn't around for her on New Year's Eve. Again, she messaged Kristin, who was planning on doing something with other friends. They were at the 'What shall we do?' stage of planning and one option was to go to a party in Pretoria, where Reeva was house-sitting for Oscar. Kristin suggested that she join them and perhaps her guy friends could also come and stay at Oscar's house for that night so they wouldn't have to drive back to Johannesburg. Reeva said no, Oscar would freak out. Kristin was irritated because it seemed *everything* with him was a drama and this was the way she had to act around him. She thought it was very rude of him to ask Reeva to look after his house over New Year's Eve and not allow anyone there to keep her company. He did not seem to care at all about her security, physical or emotional.

On New Year's Day, Reeva and Kristin had tea in the morning, pampering themselves with face masks on and they were going to go to the cinema to see *The Life of Pi*. 'In hindsight, it was so ironic,' Kristin tells me. 'I feel I have very good instincts and I just didn't have a good feeling about 2013. I said to Reeva, "I don't know why I feel like this, but I do." She said, "No, I think 2013 is going to be a great year. I can feel it . . ."'

About midday Reeva messaged me to say Oscar had bought her a plane ticket to join him in Cape Town and so she'd have to drop our plan. She said, 'This is me being spontaneous!' – which Kristin thought was strange, because it wasn't her being spontaneous. I mean, who wouldn't take the plane ticket? It wasn't spontaneity, it was Reeva jumping at Oscar's beck and call and she seemed to feel it necessary to apologise for that. She was not herself around him.

That morning of 1 January was the last time Kristin saw Reeva. That same morning she hoped it was the end of Oscar. 'She'd only known Oscar for seven weeks so it was too early for me to question her, but I had definitely decided that when "it" ended with him I was going to say that I hoped she wasn't going to go for another sports person and be the trophy girlfriend again,' she said. 'It didn't sit well with me, and after Francois too, I definitely didn't want a third one.'

New Year is a time for celebration, for looking back over the past year and making plans for the future. On a professional level, Reeva had so much to be proud of with *Tropika* set to air and a host of new projects in the pipeline. I hate to think of her spending the holiday period upset and confused. When she first moved to the city she found it a difficult environment, competitive and quite bitchy. She found happiness and a healthy equilibrium with Warren. When she travelled to Cape Town for modelling jobs, she'd say to me: 'It's very hard, leaving Warren in Johannesburg, but it's work and money.' I fear that once she'd split from him, she underestimated how lonely and vulnerable she might feel without the security of a stable loving relationship. She was big on star signs and quoting Leo traits, such as 'A Leo cannot live without love. Love is a Leo's life blood'. Reeva loved everybody and she would expect to be loved protectively by the person she herself chose to love.

Despite whatever drama was going on in her love life, it was typical of her to share only positive thoughts in seasonal greetings to her friends and Twitter followers:

Around this time 7 years ago I broke my back & learnt how to walk again. The day before Xmas, I ask u to count your blessings! Happy Holidays!

On 25 December, her greeting was:

Merry Christmas everyone and Happy Birthday to the greatest man that ever walked the Earth!! Sending Love & Light to you all xxxxx.

Reeva

On 27 December, she shared a New Year's Resolution which suggested she was determined to live according to her own values:

In 2013 I will speak my mind. Walk where my feet dream to tread. Share company with those who make my heart smile. Make my dreams a reality.

A day later, she wrote:

The soul would have no rainbow had the eyes no tears.

The next day:

I am who I am by the grace of God. Nothing more. Nothing less. If He can love me as I am, then so should you I guess. – Me

On 30 December:

Today I wish I could pick up the phone and call my grandfather. He had the answers to everything! Who would you call that you can't now?

And on New Year's Eve, when she was alone:

Going to miss some of my best people tonight @OscarPistorius @gi_myers @Iamfomo Have the most amazing night crazies! Send piccies :)

This was followed by:

About to go to sleep on this 1st day of 2013. I wish you all an incredible day, be safe & count your every blessing xxxx.

On 1 January she duly caught a flight to Cape Town to take a break with Oscar and a few friends. Kim received a phone call from Reeva asking if she wanted to do coffee. She said Ossie was taking her to Hermanus and she wondered if they could stop and have breakfast with them on the way. She suggested Ons Huisie, a café in Small Bay, Bloubergstrand, on the beach where their grandparents took them often as children and where Grandpa Alec's ashes were scattered. It was a place of special significance to the family and of historical significance too in that it overlooks Robben Island where Nelson Mandela was imprisoned for twenty-eight years.

Kim and her family were all nervous of meeting the great South African hero Oscar Pistorius, but he was the one left looking shy in the background when they turned up at Kim and Dion's house with Reeva squealing 'Kimmy!', hugging them both, and getting excited about reuniting with the girls. Reeva had told Kim that she had not had a nice Christmas and Kim, knowing how soul-destroying that would be for an occasion-loving girl like Reeva and worried that something wasn't right in the relationship, watched carefully for signs that all was well with her cousin. 'We spent about two hours together. I did think he was nice,' she said to me afterwards – because of course she was the first member of the family to meet him and we were all curious. Kim said they looked like they were happy together. There was a lot of teasing at the table about him going out on New Year's Eve and him leaving her alone, and he looked suitably sheepish, like a guilty schoolboy. Apparently, though, the service at the café was atrocious and Kim could see Oscar getting quite angry about it, but he was too polite to show his frustration in front of them. He got up and sorted it out away from the table. He also received a telephone call. Once he'd left the table, Kim took the opportunity to ask Reeva if she was happy.

'Reeva hunched up her shoulders – you could see she was excited to be in Cape Town – and said, "Yes." I could see something hesitant in her response, and she could see that I had picked that up. "We will have a chat," she said. "We'll talk about it later."

'I had expected her to say, "YES!"' said Kim. 'I thought "We'll talk later" didn't sound right — and I just wish now that I'd stopped and asked her what she meant. But there was no time.'

Reeva and Oscar continued on to Hermanus, ninety minutes southeast of Cape Town. She posted a picture of the sunrise taken from the balcony of the presidential suite at the spa hotel where they stayed. She tweeted a picture of Oscar at the wheel of an Aston Martin with the caption: **The chauffeurs in Cape Town hey. Nice!** They had lunch at Shimmy Beach Club — **Tooooo much food!!! Amazing holiday :)** — and she came back typically both thanking Cape Town and the special people who made this break memorable and noting the risk to animals of the dangerous temperatures. **So hot today WOW!!! Make sure your pets have loads of fresh water to keep them hydrated :)**

Later in January, Reeva rang me and said she had decided she was going to devote her time to Oscar. Despite the problems, she had made up her mind to give everything to the relationship and see how it went. She loved him, she assured me.

At my age I'm not someone who bothers with social media. I know it's ephemeral, of-the-moment stuff that keeps the modern world going around, but the press have made much of the tweets and posts that were exchanged between Reeva and Oscar. I look at some of her words now and I can't help but try to search for signs to analyse her feelings and interpret them as her baring her soul, even on a public forum. She described herself in professional terms on Twitter as 'SA Model, Cover Girl, Tropika Island of Treasure Celeb Contestant, Law Graduate, Child of God'. Where most of her tweets and Instagram snaps throughout 2012 had been about events, parties, products, her routine as a model and public rallies to support the causes that were important to her, increasingly, in these last three months of her life, there were verbal snippets and inspirational quotes that suggest she was having a hard time as she struggled to stabilise this fledgling relationship with Oscar. On 16 January she posts this thought:

Out of every misery, you WILL find your rainbow. A lesson. A truth. Nothing is a wasted experience if you look with willing eyes!

We learnt in court when Captain Francois Moller read out their WhatsApp exchanges that all this time she was standing her ground with a combustible personality. To hear her words read out in court when the police mobile phone analyst went through transcripts of anguished exchanges between the pair was astonishing. It was as if she was in the courtroom, giving her own evidence. Her words were so powerful, so heartfelt and eloquent in their honesty. On 27 January, just a few weeks before she died, she uploaded a collage of photos to Instagram which included the picture of her and a shirtless Oscar on the beach that she would later frame as his Valentine's Day present. She was excited about attending the engagement party of her close friend Darren Fresco and his fiancée Beatrix with Oscar.

And then this private message to Oscar:

I'm not 100% sure why I'm sitting down to type you a message first but perhaps it says a lot about what's going on here. Today was one of my best friend's engagements and I wanted to stay longer, I was enjoying myself but it's over now. You have picked on me incessantly since you got back from CT [Cape Town] and I understand that you are sick but it's nasty. Yesterday wasn't nice for either of us but we managed to pull through and communicate well enough to show our care for each other is greater than the drama that attacked us. I was not flirting with anyone today. I feel sick that you suggested that and that you made a scene at the table and made us leave early. I'm terribly disappointed in how the day ended and how you left me. We are living in a double standard relationship where you can be mad about how I deal with stuff when you are very quick to act cold and offish when you're unhappy. Every 5 seconds I hear how you dated another chick. You really have dated a lot of people yet you get upset if I mention ONE funny story with a long term boyfriend. I do everything to make you happy and to not say anything to rock the boat with u. You do everything to throw tantrums in front of people. I have been upset by you for 2 days now. I'm so upset I left Darren's party early. SO upset. I can't get that day back. I'm scared of you sometimes and how u snap at me and of how you will react to me. You make me happy 90% of the time and I think we are amazing together but I am not some other bitch you may know trying to kill your vibe. I am the girl who let go with u even when I was scared out of my mind to. I'm the girl who fell in love with u and wanted to tell u this weekend. But I'm also the girl that gets sidestepped when you are in a s**t mood. When I feel you think u have me so why try anymore. I get snapped at and told my accents and voices are annoying. I touch your neck to show u I care and you tell me to stop. Stop chewing gum. Do this don't do that. You don't want to hear stuff cut me off. Your endorsements your reputation your impression of someone innocent blown out of proportion and f***ed up a special day for me. I'm sorry if you truly felt I was hitting on my friend Sams husband and I'm sorry that u think that little of me. From the outside I think it looks like we are a struggle and maybe that's what we are. I just want to love and be loved. Be happy and make someone SO happy.

Maybe we can't do that for each other. Cos right now I know u aren't happy and I am certainly very unhappy and sad.

And just two days later, she admitted via Twitter – **Some days you just want to stay in bed and nap and think and watch tv and drink tea. It's those 'I need my mommy' days** – and a couple of days after that, she was trying to cling on to positives: **When someone has the ability to make you feel blessed every single day. #thankful #thelittlethings.**

Kristin told me that throughout January she could hardly sleep. She was so tense and she wonders to this day if she had a sense of something. She said Reeva had called to invite her to a *braai* at Oscar's house in late January, but Kristin didn't want to go. Instinctively she didn't want to become involved. 'And I am really, really glad I didn't,' she said. 'I would have slept in the same bed, used that bathroom. I am so thankful I never went to his house.'

February began with Reeva posting a brooding picture of her boyfriend with the comment, **He certainly doesn't need more followers but he's beautiful to look at & says some smart stuff too ;) @OscarPistorius**. He, on the other hand, was quoted in *Sarie* magazine explaining how difficult he found it to trust anyone: 'You're never sure in a relationship. You take a chance every time you get to know someone.'

Behind the scenes, things sound rocky. What's this about on 7 February?

When it takes you an entire day to try and compose a fitting response, a lacking one at that, rather leave it. It's just substandard.

On 8 February, in another private WhatsApp message that was read in full in court, she again objected to his behaviour towards her at a public function.

I like to believe that I made you proud when I attend these kind of functions with you. I present myself well and can converse with others while you are off busy chatting to fans and friends. I also knew people there tonight and whilst you were having one or two pics taken I was saying goodbye to the people in my industry and Fitz wanted a photo with me. I was just being cordial by saying goodbye whilst you were busy. I completely understood your desperation to leave and thought I would be helping you by getting to the exit before you because I can't rush on the heels I was wearing. I thought it would make a difference in us getting out without you getting harassed anymore. I didn't think you would criticize me for doing that especially not so loudly so that others could hear. I might joke around and be all tomboyish at times but I regard myself as a lady and I didn't feel like one tonight after the way you treated me when we left. I'm a person too and I appreciate that you invited me out tonight and I realize that you get harassed but I am trying my best to make you happy and I feel as though you sometimes never are, no matter the effort I put in. I can't be attacked by outsiders for dating you and be attacked by you – the one person I deserve protection from.

Five days before her death, the pair seemed ensconced in a routine of cosy evenings and healthy breakfasts. They had a cosy popcorn and movie night in and Reeva had retweeted a post that ran:

Relationships!@RELATIONSHIP = When you fall in love with someone's personality everything about them becomes beautiful.

On 9 February she uploaded a disturbing illustration to condemn violence against women with the comment, I woke up in a happy safe home this morning, she writes. Not everyone did. Speak out against the rape of individuals in SA. RIP Annie Booysen. #rape #crime#sayNO. The details were so horrendous and the circumstances so poignant – an adolescent girl walking home with a man for whom she harboured romantic notions – that the savage crime moved the nation to prioritise the war against rape. President Zuma condemned the attack as 'shocking, cruel and most inhumane'; the Congress of South African Trade Unions, the country's biggest labour union, called for mass action over rape in South Africa. Opposition leader Lindiwe Mazibuko called for parliamentary hearings and the United Nations issued a statement strongly condemning the rape and murder. It was the kind of incident that enraged Reeva.

On 12 February Reeva contacted her former boyfriend Warren, suggesting a quick coffee. She texted Oscar about meeting up with her ex, as if she had to ask for permission. He told her to go, saying 'I have a dentist appointment, maybe go see him and come see me when I'm done.' Warren noted that Reeva seemed happy, though he was moved to ask her if everything was all right when Oscar phoned twice in the forty minutes that they were catching up over coffee. She said everything was going well for her. But Reeva was proud, she would never have admitted to difficulties to Warren. The next day she uploaded a picture of a shake. Oscar had made her breakfast and she sounded happy:

It's a beautiful day! Make things happen. Starting my day off with a yummy healthy shake from my boo ☺ #healthyliving.

I don't know what things she made happen in her day, but she did not betray any disquiet when I spoke to her as she arrived at 286 Bushwillow Street, Silver Woods Country Estate, to cook Oscar a romantic dinner. She'd bought cooked chicken breasts, yoghurts and cheese. In her bag she had packed a specially wrapped photograph of the two of them and a Valentine's Day card. The front of the card read: 'Roses are red, violets are blue . . . ' Inside, she had written, 'I think today is a good day to tell you that . . . I love you.'

It's heartbreaking to think she would not come out of those gates alive. Her Valentine's gift and card would remain unopened for months. He did not have anything for her.

Something was not right, I'm sure. Reeva would never talk at length about their romance, but she had confided to me that she hadn't slept with him. They'd shared a bed, but she was scared to take the relationship to that level. She had only had two boyfriends, Wayne and Warren, both long-term romances of five or six years each which ended, ultimately, in friendship. She wouldn't want to sleep with

177

Oscar if she wasn't sure. I believe their relationship was coming to an end. In her heart of hearts, she didn't think it was making either of them happy. Security cameras showed Reeva smiling as she greeted the guard at the Silver Woods security gates. Scroll back a few frames on the CCTV images, though, and she looks totally miserable. Oscar arrived in his car about half an hour later. Barry and I both feel something had been brewing between them. We believe from 1 a.m. they were fighting – as vouched by the neighbour who said they heard a couple arguing. There is no doubt in our minds that something went horribly wrong, something upset her so terribly that she hid behind a locked door with two mobile phones. We're sure there's more to the story than what Oscar has produced so far. Four mobile phones were found in the bathroom, suggesting that either of them could have received a Valentine's Day message from another admirer that might have sparked a row. Her clothes were packed. There is no doubt in our minds: she had decided to leave Oscar that night.

Three Months With Oscar

Open letter to Oscar Pistorius from Sheena Jonker, Human Rights Activist:

Dear Oscar

I have wanted to write to you for some time. I think the time is now.

I am sorry that you are going through what you are. I am sorry that Reeva lost her life in such a violent way. I am sorry she lost her life at all. I am sorry that, whatever the circumstances, you were ultimately the one who ended a beautiful life. And now your life (which cannot be viewed separate from your freedom) is on the line. And so are the lives of many that are subject to perpetual cycles of violence. And now, indeed, the profile of our beautiful country itself is on the line.

Here is the truth: at this point, no one knows the truth, but you. You are the custodian of what really happened on the night of Valentine's day last year.

All I can say is that you have a story to tell. Tell it with courage. Take South African Society into your confidence. Take the world into your confidence. Tell that story. Don't hold back. The truth has high value, and it is ultimately the truth that sets us free.

If you have advisors that are helping you to advance a version that could fit with (possibly compromised) forensics. If you know that that version is actually untrue, rise up in courage and tell the truth. Violence, especially that against women and children, is a problem for us all. And we all need to be part of the solution. The bare, raw, painful truth of what happened on that night, told out of a place of courage, has so much power to transform the problem we have. Your story has the power to change many lives. Your story has the power to save many lives. Your story, told truthfully, has the power to save your own life. Set you free.

If you are surrounded by brilliant advisors that are, as they ethically can, 'testing the state case', tactically playing an artificial rules-based evidence system that is susceptible to muting or shutting down massive tracts of truth, don't. Don't partake in playing a system where you know you can win, but you were wrong. A system, where you can be right in the argument, but wrong in substance. That's not justice.

As I said earlier, you are the custodian of the truth here. Only you. The stakes are high. You have a responsibility based on who you are as a human, and the profile you have internationally, to steward that truth. It will take strength and courage.

All of us are capable of harm. All of us are capable of ending lives even. If I make a call to eat a burger whilst driving my car, for instance I can end a life in an instant. Or many lives. Your story and the circumstances are obviously very different. Each of us have capacity for harm in different ways and to various degrees. But let's talk about it. Let's know the truth, as ugly and as painful as it may be. And then let's decide, as a society, as humanity, how we go about using the cold hard truth to transform. To heal.

But don't look around for others to blame. That's what cowards do. And you have shown that you have the capacity for great courage in many ways. Don't make South Africa the fall guy. Don't bring more harm to an already harmed situation. Don't be that guy, Oscar. Much is at stake. And the whole world is watching.

It's not too late. It's not too late to be everything you were destined to be. Take courage. Rise up. Be strong. Tell your story. Be that guy. Be the guy that tells the truth, no matter how hard. And is willing to do whatever it takes to clean up the mess. Who knows, you may just change the world, starting with your own life.

Be that guy, Oscar.

Peace.

Sheena Jonker

The Trial

For more than a year I had been trying to work out the emotional background to my daughter's needless violent death: what had been going on in her life that she could end up in such a situation with such a man? On 3 March 2014, it was time for the official truth-seeking process to begin at the North Gauteng High Court in Pretoria. I had been warned I'd find the trial a 'trial' in every sense of the word, but, comfortingly, public opinion too was willing the truth to emerge. Here, at last, we hoped to resolve the mystery of how our polished, organised and self-possessed daughter came to meet such a messy end, leaving so many unanswered questions. On the day the news of her death broke, her close friends had all called each other to find out if she'd confided anything to anyone that might shed light on what had happened, but, although everyone knew Oscar had a temper, no one knew of anything that could have triggered such an escalation. We all wanted answers.

To understand the process, I took it day by day, fact by fact, starting from the moment Oscar Pistorius was sensationally charged with Reeva's murder on 15 February 2013. Later that year, he appeared in court again for a bail hearing and then an indictment hearing; both sessions in court yielded details which would become significant points in the trial as the state opened its case against him.

During the bail hearing on 19 February – the day on which we held Reeva's funeral service – both the prosecution led by Gerrie Nel and the defence stated that Oscar had fired four shots through a locked toilet door, hitting Reeva three times. Gerrie Nel claimed that Oscar had put on his prosthetic legs, walked across his bedroom to the bathroom and intentionally shot Reeva through the door. He argued that the time taken to pick up the gun, put on his legs and walk down the corridor was enough to establish the murder as premeditated. The defence team, meanwhile, said Pistorius did not put on his prosthetics and claimed that he thought Reeva was in bed and that the person in the toilet was an intruder. The bail hearing went on for four days and set out the basic positions of both camps. The chief investigating officer, Hilton Botha – the policeman who had called

me that terrible morning to tell me my daughter was dead – told of a witness who had heard gunshots coming from Oscar's house, followed by a female screaming and then further gunshots. He said the trajectory of the gunshots indicated they had been fired downward and directly toward the toilet. On 22 February the bail hearing ended with Chief Magistrate Desmond Nair concluding that the state had not convinced him that Pistorius posed a flight risk and that bail could be fixed at one million rand.

On the same day, we learnt Botha was to be removed from the case following revelations that he was facing attempted murder charges dating from an incident in 2009. He was replaced by Vineshkumar Moonoo, the most senior detective in the South African Police Service. Six months later, on 19 August – when we should have been celebrating Reeva's thirtieth birthday, a day which instead we spent quietly with Michael and Lyn – Oscar attended Pretoria Magistrates' Court again to be served with an indictment for murder, plus an additional charge of illegal possession of ammunition. On 20 November, he was served with new indictment papers containing the two extra charges of firing a gun in a public space.

The trial was set to take place from 3–20 March, and later extended to 16 May. Within that period, the court was set to adjourn after proceedings on 17 April, returning on 5 May,

to accommodate scheduling conflicts of the prosecution. Each proposed re-scheduling drew out the sense of the big ordeal facing us. I was anticipating a long haul. The trial was assigned to Judge Thokozile Matilda Masipa, who then appointed two assessors, Janette Henzen du Toit and Themba Mazibuko, to flank her on the bench and help evaluate the evidence presented by prosecution and defence in order to reach a verdict. We just had to live in limbo and await the start of the trial. On 25 February 2014, Judge President Dunstan Mlambo ruled that the entire trial could be broadcast live via audio and that parts of the trial could be broadcast live via television – namely the opening and closing arguments, the testimony of consenting state witnesses, the judgement, and the sentencing, if applicable. I was still in two minds about the televisation process. The media attention and consequent public hunger for more analysis and comment about the case would make it a much bigger ordeal for us, but I hoped the spotlight would also highlight the unsavoury issue of gun violence and help precipitate some positive outcome for society.

When Masipa was announced as the judge, I read her whole life story. The judge and the assessors would decide if Oscar Pistorius intentionally killed our daughter or if he genuinely thought she was an intruder and thereby killed her by accident. South Africa does not have trials by jury because it

Reeva's teenage paintings that now seem so prophetic

Reeva's first *FHM* cover – another proud moment for us all

Reeva's modelling was going
from strength to strength.
Above, a beauty shoot in 2004;
below, in a campaign for Pallu
evening dresses

Reeva with Abby at her family farm in December 2010, drinking champagne and fruit juice. This is the last Christmas they spent together.

With other dear friends, Kristin and Beatrix on New Years Eve, 2012, when she was looking after the house in Johannesburg. Whatever was going on in her life, Reeva always stayed close to her friends

Reeva with the cake she baked at the BBC Lifestyle launch of 'Bake-Off' in South Africa

On her visit to the Kitty and Puppy Haven in Johannesburg in January 2013

Reeva and Oscar on their first date together at the South African Sports Awards 2012

Together again in January 2013, just before her death

Arriving in court with Dup, our advocate. The media frenzy around the trial was unlike anything I'd ever experienced before

With Barry at the trial

Only one person really knows what happened to Reeva that night, but my beautiful daughter will always be in my heart

is nearly impossible to find jurors who have not been influenced by the racial effects of apartheid. I was curious to find out as much as I could about her.

The first thing I noticed was that she is exactly the same age as me and that gave me a good feeling about her. She is a mother and a grandmother as well, I thought. As a High Court judge, she has a reputation for being extremely thorough and fair to everyone – and for having no mercy for abusive men. Famously, she had handed down a life sentence to policeman Freddy Mashamba for shooting and killing his wife, Rudzani Ramango, in a row over their divorce settlement, concluding that he was not above the law and that he was a killer, not a protector like he was supposed to be. In another case, she sentenced serial rapist and robber, Shepherd Moyo, to 252 years in jail after he was arrested and tried following a seven-year crime spree. She told him she was troubled by his lack of remorse.

Judge Masipa comes from Soweto, the township famous for the anti-apartheid youth uprisings in the 1980s. Her mother died when the family were still young and she had to support them. Despite those responsibilities, she was determined to do something with her own life. She was born in 1947, one year before apartheid, or racial segregation, became an official ideology that was supported by a leading political party in the 1948 political elections. In 1974, she received a

Bachelor of Arts degree, specialising in social work, and worked in the townships with women challenged by poverty, apartheid issues and domestic violence. She felt the need to air the injustices she witnessed on a daily basis and began a career as a journalist. In the mid-1970s she was arrested after demonstrating with fellow women journalists against the apartheid regime's attempts to suppress a newspaper she worked on – and spent a night in jail. Working as a crime reporter for *The World*, *Post* and *The Sowetan* newspapers ignited her interest in law which she set out to pursue as a career. Her background and motivation to go into law resonated with me, too, as I felt it echoed Reeva's long-term ambition to use her public profile to highlight injustices.

In 1990, the same year that Nelson Mandela was released from prison, Masipa received a law degree from the University of South Africa and in her late forties began practising as an advocate. In 1998, she became the second black woman to be appointed a judge in the High Court of South Africa, following Constitutional Court judge Yvonne Mokgoro and High Court judge Lucy Mailula. Today, she is still part of a minority as one of 76 female judges in a pool of 239. Much was made of her selection for the trial against Oscar Pistorius – not least the fact that her courtroom would mirror modern South African society with a Zulu judge raised in a township presiding over two Afrikaner lawyers and a wealthy Afrikaner accused – but the Department of Justice insisted the appointment was a routine allocation of court cases and not a special selection. Would her perspective nevertheless prove crucial?

Gerrie Nel, a state prosecutor and advocate for the National Prosecuting Authority known as 'the pitbull pros-ecutor', was the leading the state's case. He was our man. I found him very charismatic when we'd met in Dup's cham-bers. Gerrie came to Port Elizabeth with the investigating officer, Captain Mike van Aardt – who had already been to see Barry and I at home to say that he'd taken the case and reassure us that he was going to pursue it as if it were his own daughter. They told us they'd interviewed 107 witnesses and not one had a bad word to say about Reeva. Lawyer friends told us Gerrie had more than thirty years' experience and often took on high-profile cases, prosecuting with flair, ded-ication and determination. In contrast to Gerrie, who is paid a state salary, the defence team was rumoured to be costing Oscar Pistorius R100,000 per day; they were led by Barry Roux SC, a senior advocate of the Johannesburg Bar renowned for his skill in cross-examination and his ability to unsettle witnesses.

To take up our seats that rainy and depressing Monday, 382 days after we lost Reeva, Simone, Jennifer and I had flown up the previous evening from Port Elizabeth with Dup and his

wife Truia. We'd settled in at the guest house and rallied ourselves for Day 1 of the trial. I had asked for a wake-up call at
5 a.m. – not that I would sleep well anyway – and tried to
force down some breakfast and get ready for the twenty-
minute drive to the High Court. I kept my emotions in check
by concentrating on trivial things like what to wear. Respectful for court, I dressed in a black blazer, trousers, a white top
and Reeva's pearl necklace; Simone and Jennifer also wore
sombre black. We had to park quite a way from the High
Court building and walk down the pavement with the full
glare of the world's media pressing in on us. I held on to Dup's
arm as he tried to keep an umbrella stable above our heads. A
short walk has never seemed so long with all the cameras
clicking, TV equipment whirring and reporters announcing
our arrival live into microphones as we approached.

Dup led us to courtroom GD, one of four courtrooms on
the ground floor which open out from a dimly lit, low-
ceilinged corridor. We were among the first to arrive in the
square red-brick interior. I took in the recessed white-tile
roof, fluorescent lighting and grey carpet-tiled floor that
would become a horribly familiar environment over the
coming months, and noted how the judge's raised dais faced
rows of long wooden benches like pews in a church. We filed
in to the front bench allocated for VIPs, the Steenkamp
family and friends. Kim and Dion arrived to support us.

Reeva's friend Gina Myers and her parents, Cecil and Desi, came too. Along the other half of the bench sat the Pistorius family, Oscar's uncle Arnold and aunt Lois, his aunt Sonia Grobler, his brother Carl and sister Aimee.

I was steeling myself for the moment I would see Oscar for myself for the first time in person; I wanted to look him in the eye. I'd played through this scenario in my mind a hundred times over, but without an ending. How would I feel?

Oscar arrived, dressed in a dark suit, white shirt and black tie, and walked straight past us, looking resolutely ahead. I was disappointed. I wanted to see him and I wanted him to see me, but he didn't acknowledge me. The whole point was that he must see that I was there. I'm Reeva's mother and, you know, what he did to her was terrible. I wanted him to see that I was there representing Reeva.

The trial was scheduled to start at half past nine. It got to ten o'clock, then half past ten, eleven o'clock, half past eleven, and nothing had happened. Imagine the restlessness. Everyone was walking up and down. Word came through that the court staff were looking for an Afrikaans interpreter. In South Africa, the court uses English and interpreters are called for witnesses who speak Xhosa or Afrikaans. The interpreter they had been waiting for was still occupied in an upstairs courtroom. They'd requested another at short notice from Johannesburg, and she would have to drive to Pretoria, which on a good run takes about forty minutes. Two hours in and there was no official signal that proceedings were about to begin. A whisper went around that the courtroom staff had lost the key for the door through which Judge Masipa and her assessors enter the courtroom from her chambers. They couldn't come into court because they were locked out! Jennifer whispered to me, 'They've lost the key.' I didn't believe her at first. People were saying, 'Shall we phone Houdini?' You couldn't have made it up. Eventually the call came to be upstanding as the judge climbed the steps to her black swivel chair on the bench and we bowed to her and sat down, waiting expectantly. Everything went wrong. The interpreter arrived, but broke down in tears, over-whelmed by the case, and had to leave the court. After all that! It was tempting to laugh – to relieve the tension – but we couldn't laugh in court. Good gracious.

And then we were under way. The first shock came when Judge Masipa addressed 'the accused' and asked, 'Mr Pistorius, how do you plead on premeditated murder?'

Not guilty.

How did he plead on the other three counts? *Not Guilty. Not Guilty. Not Guilty.*

I was so shocked that he was actually standing there saying *Not Guilty* to every single charge. How could he say that when Reeva is dead and he shot her? Then I realised he was saying he was not guilty of the specific charge of premeditated murder – because he would be in jail for at least thirty years if he was found guilty of that – but I did expect him to take some responsibility, not deny *everything* so emphatically when there were so many close witnesses to two of the firearms charges. I couldn't believe it. Then he accused the prosecution of attempting a character assassination, and denied that he and Reeva had been arguing.

The prosecution called the first witness. It was time to hear what other people had to say. First on the stand was a neighbour, the lady who had described hearing a woman's 'blood-curdling' screams followed by four gunshots. Michelle Burger told the court: 'The evening was extremely traumatic. The fear in that woman's voice was difficult to explain.' The information she had to impart was brief, but the court procedures meant she was in the stand a considerable time.

At the end of the day, I was numb. It was still raining as we left the court building and I was standing holding an umbrella at one of the bus stops outside the main entrance to the building when I saw the Pistorius family waiting to see Oscar safely through the sea of media. They came over to me. One of his aunts squeezed my arm and the other reached out and clasped my hand. Then Oscar's older brother, Carl, came up and hugged me. He held his cheek against mine without saying a word. I didn't mind that. You've got to feel for them too. They were in as much pain as I am, especially the little sister Aimee. Reeva was her friend, you know. She said to me, Reeva was always at their house and they had such fun. I felt sorry for the family. I have no hate in my heart. Not one of them pulled the trigger, yet everyone close to Oscar was going through a traumatic time.

So it was over. We had attended the first day of *The State vs Oscar Pistorius* as Dup had suggested and then he said I must go home, kindly reminding me that I didn't have to put myself through that every day.

Back at home in Port Elizabeth, I watched every minute of the next few days of the trial on television. I saw Michelle Burger break down in tears and insist she was being as honest as she could be when the defence questioned her credibility. She sounded haunted by what she'd heard, saying every time she showered now she remembers the terrifying screams she heard. The proceedings were briefly adjourned when the court was told a media outlet was broadcasting an image of Michelle Burger, despite her request not to have her image shown, and that made me value the selflessness of these people who had come forward to do their civic duty and tell what they had seen and heard. I learnt that Estelle van der Merwe, also a neighbour of Oscar's, heard arguing for about an hour before the shooting noises. Often, the television cameras flitted back to focus on 'the accused' as he held his head in his hands and wiped away tears as a description of Reeva's grievous injuries was read out.

The next day, sitting on our red sofa under a giant black-and-white photograph of Reeva circled by handwritten messages from her friends, I kept track of the testimonies of further witnesses: professional boxer Kevin Lerena told a hushed court how Oscar had asked a friend to take the blame for shooting a gun in a restaurant last year. Even through the TV screen I could sense the trauma that everyone involved in the case was suffering. Another witness, neighbour Charl Johnson, said he had received phone calls and a threat after his phone number was read out in court the previous day. He continued to give evidence, describing how he heard a woman's cries and gunshots. In cross-examination, Barry Roux suggested Johnson and his wife, Michelle Burger, had colluded over their testimony, but they stuck to their story. They knew what they had heard. I could see now how it was going to go – like a seesaw. Nel, then Roux. Nel, then Roux. The dynamic is up and down as each side compete to claim the most persuasive argument. One line of questioning seeks to dig out the truth we want; the other is negative for us. For a victim's family, the adversarial nature of the criminal justice system is tough on the emotions. Watching the toing and froing made me want to transplant myself back into courtroom GD. It came to me that it was wrong to be back at home watching it on TV. This was all about seeing justice done for our daughter. I said to Barry, 'I have to go back. I can't sit here. I'm not in the right place. I have to be there for her.'

Dup was less than thrilled by my decision. As a senior counsel, he has worked on many murder cases and he knew exactly what I would have to go through. But I insisted. I intended to be there every day. While Jacqui Mofokeng and her ladies helped make arrangements for my return to Pretoria, emotions ran high in the courtroom on the fourth day. Johan Stipp, another neighbour of Oscar's who is also a doctor, described what he saw. The first witness on the scene, he said he heard male and female voices 'intermingled', and said: 'The first thing he [Oscar] said was, "I shot her. I thought she was a burglar. I shot her,"' adding that Oscar was 'very upset'. Dr Stipp disagreed with the defence's theory that he heard a cricket bat hitting the bathroom door, rather than gunshots. He said he heard three gunshots, followed by a woman screaming, then two or three more gunshots. Barry Roux pounced on this saying it contradicted the forensic evidence.

I was back in court on the day Oscar greeted the ANCWL ladies as he entered. These were the ladies who sung in protest outside the High Court, recognisable in their long green shirts over black skirts or trousers. The look on their faces as he spoke to them was one of utter amazement. It was no easier facing the ordeal of coming into court on this second visit, but I had started to take pills to keep control. Your stomach gets tied in knots with stress so I took Immodium to calm it. You didn't want to be sitting there, cramping, and having to rush out of court. I also took a mild 0.25mg tranquilliser to keep my mood steady because I could never anticipate what emotion each minute of testimony would prompt. Early on, the Silver Woods security guard Pieter Baba revealed Oscar called him and said through tears that everything was fine. Fine? How could everything be fine when my daughter was lying in his house lifeless?

Next up was Samantha Taylor, Oscar's previous girlfriend, who got on the stand and said Oscar cheated on her with Reeva. She seemed so painfully young and she just blurted it out. She also witnessed his gun being waved around, testifying how he shot through the open sunroof of a car. The defence suggested Oscar was vulnerable and scared of being attacked, but Samantha Taylor said no, he always carried a gun without being overly anxious or concerned about his safety. She added that he also took his mobile phone to bed every night – which made me wonder again why, if we were to believe his story about an intruder, he didn't just phone the police or security that night, instead of approaching his perceived 'intruder' with a gun. She also disagreed with the defence that her boyfriend's screams could be mistaken for a woman and crucially, I felt, revealed there were one or two occasions when Oscar had thought he heard an intruder in the night and had woken her up.

A new week, and it began horribly. I have been so lucky to have the support of friends such as Dup and Jennifer as well as family. Reeva, I will always be haunted to know, died a terrible, painful death and pathologist Gert Saayman stepped forward to give his testimony of the autopsy. The details were so graphic the judge banned live broadcast and reporting of the testimony to preserve Reeva's dignity, allowing only summary evidence to be reported later on. Professor Saayman explained that the bullets fired by Oscar 'mushroomed' on impact and were designed to cause maximum damage. He detailed each of the wounds Reeva suffered from these gunshots – to her hip and thigh, arm, head and fingers, and said she would have been immediately brain-damaged, and unconscious, but did not necessarily die straight away. He pinpointed the bullet holes in her Nike shorts and sleeveless black top. Throughout the testimony Oscar was audibly dry retching and vomiting, just feet from us. It wasn't very nice. His fingers were in his ears so he couldn't hear. It was a circus. The pathologist added an interesting fact: he said Reeva's last meal was at 1 a.m., about two hours before she died, which contradicted Oscar's story that they were both in bed from 10 p.m. The next day Professor Saayman stuck to his conclusion under cross-examination.

Darren Fresco was the next witness called – a good friend of Reeva's and also of Oscar's. It was at his engagement party that Oscar caused the scene that prompted one of Reeva's long, anguished WhatsApp messages about how she was scared of him and the way he snapped at her. His wife Beatrix has had a huge tattoo spelling out REEVA on her back in memory of her. They loved her, you know. They came to her funeral. I'd met Darren before with Reeva for coffee, in a fun context. Now I was seeing all her friends again, but in stressful circumstances. Those four shots in the night have affected all these young peoples' lives. Darren was phoning me all the time after her death, he was so upset, and I had to tell him I couldn't speak to him; I didn't know if he was still on friendly terms with Oscar or not. But he wasn't. He had already given evidence against him on two of the firearm charges, testifying how Oscar had shot a gun out of the sunroof of a car and how on another occasion Oscar took his Glock 27 pistol, knowing it was 'one-up', i.e. had a bullet in it, and let off a shot before asking Darren to take the blame. It was brave of Darren to give evidence. He was promised indemnity from prosecution if his evidence proved reliable.

By this stage Jennifer and I had got into a routine. We shared a suite at the guest house, waking up early every morning to have coffee on the balcony and let Jennifer have a smoke. The guest house was located in a beautiful area with jacaranda-lined streets and lush gardens where birdsong and the sound of barking dogs fills the air. Sometimes I'd wake to find a white feather on the balcony. 'Reeva's here,' I'd call to Jennifer. It always cheered me to receive a little sign from her in heaven.

It was killing Barry to stay at home. He was watching every minute on TV but I was comforted to think that he could get up and walk out of the room when it all became too much for him. Simone decided not to come again after the first day. I wouldn't let her. She's not strong enough for this sort of ordeal. Dup came as often as he could with his wife Truia. They're very warm and loving people. Kim came when she could too, with her husband Dion, but she has a growing family, one daughter doing matriculation and stuff, but I appreciated her support so much. She and Reeva were very close. She told me she just looked at her one day and realised there was something special about her, like she was an angel – she was so sensitive to other people's needs. Jacqui Mofokeng and the four ladies from the Women's League maintained a permanent vigil with me too.

I was warned that the next tranche of evidence would

come with a reconstruction in the courtroom of the bath-room where Reeva was shot. Colonel Vermeulen, a forensic investigator who examined the scene, was due to answer questions on his findings. The bathroom was a huge con-struction, almost blocking our view of the witness stand, but it was heartbreaking to see the size of the toilet cubicle. She had no space that night, nowhere to go. How he could say the person inside the toilet was the aggressor, opening the door to come and get him, I don't know. Whoever was in that space was at a disadvantage, as good as cornered. It was the actual door and right there in front of me were the four bullet holes labelled A B C and D. Oh, it was horrendous to see that and I slightly lost track of what was being debated about whether Oscar was wearing his prosthetic legs, or not, when he broke down the toilet door.

The week continued to be hard to endure. Day 9 ushered in the testimony of the first police officer to arrive at Oscar's house and he described in detail the crime scene. I was extremely disturbed by the graphic nature of some of the court images of the crime scene   guns, bullet casings, pools of blood and phones strewn on the floor. Of course I was. I felt utterly sick. This was my daughter's blood, her life-sap-ping injuries. Sitting through this part of the testimony was the hardest part. It sapped my strength. I couldn't look. I would have to be sub-human to look at my child's injuries.

It was horrendous because it brought back the agony of knowing what a horrible, painful death she suffered. And then there was Oscar, sobbing uncontrollably and throwing up in his green plastic bucket. Jacqui Mofokeng complained to Gerrie Nel and insisted that I must have some warning before these images were projected on the screen. He agreed to turn his head and give me a signal so that I could leave the court or take off my glasses or lower my eyes. I understood people must see the injuries and horrific bloodshed he caused, but if it's your daughter, you don't want to see it. Colonel Vermeulen was grilled by Barry Roux, who was intent on questioning police procedures in the handling of evidence.

Gerrie Nel was concerned about me during this stage of the trial and I duly developed a tactic of lowering my eyes on his signal. Unfortunately, I did actually see one gruesome image by mistake – Oscar standing on his prosthetic legs, with no top on, drenched in Reeva's blood. It was spooky, macabre. He was standing there looking like a mad person. That image will never go away. That was when he lifted her down the stairs. Why did he do that? Why did he move her when she was so grievously injured?

It was a gruelling week, totally wearing. Each day I'd emerge from court and it felt as if I'd been running on a treadmill for four days. Every three days or so it would catch up with me. I'd be drained. It was the concentration and the struggle to remain composed in the emotional spotlight that took so much out of me. I would get quite nervous about how I would cope each day. The eleventh day – when police photographer Bennie van Staden was due to show more graphic images of blood stains and firearms trainer Sean Rens testified that Oscar had a thorough knowledge of laws detailing when someone can draw a gun on an intruder – started very stressfully. We had to park quite a way from the court and walk in past all the media tents with whirring generators and cables and wires lying across the pavement. Whenever the photographers saw me, they'd go mad and on this particular morning I was so distracted, lost in my thoughts, that I tripped over some wires and fell flat on the ground. And then Jennifer fell on top of me. We laughed about it later, but can you imagine the indignity? The TV people came out and apologised profusely. They were very nice and assured us they hadn't taken any photographs or filmed the fall. I'd grazed my hands and knees on the cement and I was quite badly shaken. A toilet roll was produced to help me clean up and then of course we had to walk across the road as cool as cucumbers to approach the main entrance and the full throng of reporters. Luckily, none of them had seen our fall. By the time I took up my place on the bench in court, I was finished. And then Oscar walked past and, on this day of all days, he stopped and said, 'Good morning, Mrs Steenkamp'. I didn't answer. I couldn't say a word. I was even more in shock. I wasn't ready to be on jolly terms with him. My way of coping was to cut myself off from him.

The firearms trainer's evidence shocked me. Oscar had four guns, he said, and at least a further six on order, including a machine gun type of weapon. What do you need a cache of guns like that for? He wasn't a dealer. That is somebody who is obsessed with guns. Then I saw pictures of him, sitting in front of a carcass of an elephant, with his uncle and grandfather holding guns. So that's how he's been brought up, killing animals. It made me even more dismayed that Reeva was with him because when Warren, her ex, began to organise shooting trips for tourists, she was horrified.

I managed to return to court the next day. During one short adjournment, Jennifer went out for a smoke and Oscar's uncle, Arnold Pistorius – in whose house he stays while on bail – came over and spoke to me. He said something about being sorry for my loss and then said, indicating his own family, 'We're just fighting for a life here,' meaning Oscar's life. And that seemed so tactless. I mean, what about Reeva's life? It's gone already. I was so shocked I couldn't say anything. I couldn't give him any warmth or anything.

A room was made available to us upstairs next to Gerrie Nel's chamber where we could go for tea and coffee during the short adjournments. We learnt to take a packed lunch to eat there, too, during the break because it proved impossible to go out for a bite and escape the court environment. We tried early on to pop out for lunch, but Jennifer and I got smacked in the face with a camera. It was a frenzy out there, you know, and they'd go mad when they spotted Oscar and his family, or us, coming in or out of court. So every day we had to remember to take in our picnic of crackers, made up by the guest-house kitchen. The trial did not allow for comfort eating. You're not very active when you're sitting all day in court. Jennifer and I had to go on a diet – or else it would have to be five times around the shopping mall for exercise!

One day Jennifer and I found all these little white feathers under the open window in our room next to Gerrie's. A white dove came and sat on the windowsill. It was breathtaking. I felt it had flown there just for us; it was a sign from Reeva and I took a photograph of it to keep. I couldn't tell everyone because they'd think I was going mad – in fact I did tell Jacqui Mofokeng and she was quite shocked. When we left court that day, the dove was still sitting there peacefully. Quite often, though, our room was locked and we ended up in Gerrie's room with his team and the investigating officers. They would offer us tea and coffee. By this stage Gerrie had become a media star. At the beginning it was Barry Roux who had all the attention, women asking for his autograph and so on, but now everyone was in love with Gerrie, even though he didn't court the limelight. Every time we saw him in his office he was busy at his desk, preparing papers and tactics for the next session in court.

On 19 March, Day 13 of the trial, I arrived as usual just before 9 a.m. and sat in between Jennifer and one of the lovely ANC Women's League ladies. Shortly before the proceedings got under way, the ANCWL lady passed me a handwritten note from Aimee Pistorius, Oscar's sister. Out of the corner of my eye, I'd seen her standing with her brother, writing something down shortly after they arrived, but I didn't imagine it was for me. It was so amusing because, of course, all the journalists sitting behind me picked up on it. Everyone wanted to know what the letter said. I refused to disclose its contents and it became this big mystery. *The letter. The letter.* I'd hear the whispers of the press people speculating on it. The saga went on for days afterwards. What Aimee actually wrote was that she had wanted to say hello to me early in the morning but that the court was already busy and she couldn't come and talk to me privately. She wanted to know if we needed anything and she included her phone number. She said the offer came from her heart. It seemed a sweet gesture, but it would not have been proper to accept their family's show of concern. I asked my niece Kim to call Aimee and explain I couldn't enter into conversation with her because it could be interpreted by others as a tactic from the Pistorius side. It was nothing personal. A law trial is an adversarial exercise susceptible to tactical game-playing. She didn't approach me again.

Judge Masipa adjourned the case until the following Monday, 24 March, in the middle of testimony about Reeva's position when she was shot. I flew home to Port Elizabeth with the very image Reeva painted on her teenage canvas whirling in my head: of herself in a defensive position with her hands over her head. According to ballistics expert, Captain Christian Mangena, this was her stance when hit by the third and fourth bullets.

This unexpected adjournment prolonged the awfulness – and it was the first of what would turn out to be six adjournments during the trial, not including the break between Closing Arguments and Delivery of Verdict, and the further four weeks until sentencing. Logistically this was also a nightmare for Jacqui Mofokeng, who insisted on sorting the flight, accommodation and car details for me each time I had to travel between Port Elizabeth and Pretoria. Those ANCWL ladies were amazing. I genuinely appreciated their warm-hearted support and presence in court. There was one lady so old her hair was almost totally grey and she'd sit there sometimes and nod off to sleep. I was thinking, 'Ooh, that's not right in court', but then I pictured her life as a granny, as the head of a family, and realised she'd probably walked a long way each morning just to be in court. She would have got up very early to feed her extended family and pack their lunches; after she'd walked home she'd have to cook supper, do the washing by hand, clean, look after her children and grand-children. She had a hard life. Of course she was exhausted, but still she came to support me, a fellow woman, and add her presence to the numbers opposing gun violence in South Africa.

Jacqui introduced me to quite a sisterhood of bereaved mothers whom she supports, particularly Busi Khumalo, the mother of Zanele Khumalo, a pregnant teenager who was raped and murdered by her boyfriend, and Sharon Saincic, the mother of Chanelle Henning, a nursery school teacher who was executed in front of her young son by two hitmen while she was in the middle of a custody battle with her ex-husband. Both understand the agony of losing a daughter in violent circumstances, how you carry a crushing ache deep in your chest that never lifts. I appreciated how both came to sit in court to support me during the case. We all felt for each other in a way only we could understand. One day, Jacqui wanted me to console Busi Khumalo, who was somewhere else in the High Court building. She led me to meet her in a private chamber, but news of this was leaked. Cameras fol-lowed us, burst into the room and took photographs. Jennifer had to run from court to court, looking for the reporters who had snatched photographs. She found the lady from *Pretoria News* who was very nice but said she'd already put it out on Twitter. I understood the media's job was to add resonance to the story, but that kind of frenzy and drama was emotionally exhausting.

For me, the most heart-wrenching day was when Captain Francois Moller, the police mobile phone expert, read out text messages between Reeva and Oscar. It was like Reeva had walked into the court. I could hear her voice and her emotional dismay so clearly in the message she sent to Oscar on 19 January 2013: **I am scared of you sometimes and how u snap at me and of how you will react to me.** It was like she was there giving evidence herself. I felt her presence so strongly. Another from Oscar to Reeva was about the shooting at Tasha's restaurant – a charge he had denied – and revealed his overriding concern for his image: **Angel please don't say a thing to anyone. Darren told everyone it was his fault. I can't afford for that to come out. The guys promised not to say a thing.**

The next day, the seesaw tipped the other way again. Barry Roux argued that only several of the hundreds of messages showed evidence of arguing. I wanted to stand up and say, but it is not the number of messages that are important, it is the weight of the words within them: **Right now I know u aren't**

happy and I am certainly very unhappy and sad, she had written. More little snippets came back to me: **I get snapped at and told my accents and voices are annoying. I touch your neck to show u I care and you tell me to stop. Stop chewing gum. Do this don't do that.** And again: **I am trying my best to make you happy and I feel as though you sometimes never are, no matter the effort I put in. I can't be attacked by outsiders for dating you and be attacked by you – the one person I deserve protection from.** These messages did not come in one 'bad phase' of their relationship; they punctuated their relationship, and had increased in frequency towards the end.

There was further dispute about whether Oscar was wearing his prosthetic legs or not when he broke down the toilet door and then, after fifteen harrowing days, the prosecution rested its case. The court was adjourned for another four days and when we returned Judge Masipa immediately postponed the trial until 7 April, as one of her assessors was too ill to come to court. We left with the prospect that on our return Oscar Pistorius himself would take the stand as the defence began its case.

On Monday 7 April, Oscar took the witness stand. We'd been warned as a family through the lawyers shortly beforehand that he intended to make a public apology. He turned and faced us for the first time in seventeen days of court proceedings and for the first time in the fourteen months since he took our daughter from us.

'My lady, may I please start my evidence by tendering an apology,' he said in a whisper. 'I would like to take this opportunity to apologise to Mr and Mrs Steenkamp, to Reeva's family, to those of you who knew her who are here today' – and he promptly broke down in tears.

I knew it was coming, so I had steeled myself to hold it together, to remain composed. The judge asked him to speak louder. 'I beg your pardon, my lady, I'll speak up,' he continued. 'I'd like to apologise and say that there's not a moment, and there hasn't been a moment, since this tragedy happened that I haven't thought about your family. I wake up every morning and you're the first people I think of, the first people I pray for. I can't imagine the pain and the sorrow and the emptiness that I've caused you and your family. I was simply trying to protect Reeva. I can promise that when she went to bed that night she felt loved. I've tried to put my words on paper many, many times to write to you, but no words will ever suffice.'

It was an extraordinary moment. You could cut the atmosphere in the courtroom with a knife: silence, but for the sound of journalists tapping on their screens. It put me in an awkward position. Why decide to say sorry to me in a televised trial in front of the whole world? I was unmoved by his apology. I felt if I melted – which would be my nature – and if I appeared to be sorry for him at this stage of his trial on the charge of premeditated murder, it would in the eyes of others lessen the awfulness of what he had done. He was in the box trying to save his own skin after he had killed my daughter and I was sitting in that courtroom waiting to hear factual truth, not to see emotions cloud the truth.

'Why are you doing this in public?' Gerrie demanded. 'It's not a thing to do in public. You could have approached Mrs Steenkamp privately through lawyers.' In the break, my advocate Dup told Gerrie that early on his representatives did contact us, but neither Barry nor I were ready. We put that on record in court.

Oscar spent five days giving evidence and, for me, it was the most interesting phase of the trial. I studied him intently and listened to my instinct about whether he was telling the truth. All the time I found myself looking towards him to see his reaction to questions. I couldn't help myself, even though I didn't want to fixate on him. He told the court he was on anti-depressants, suffered from terrible nightmares and did not want to ever hold a gun again. But he had to say that, didn't he? Most of the first day was spent discussing his childhood and school days, a boat accident, and occasions when he had been a victim of crime. It was Barry Roux, his lawyer, trying to make him feel comfortable on the witness stand, building up a sympathetic picture of him for the judge.

We came back to court the next day and sat through Oscar's explanations of the context of the WhatsApp messages the pair had exchanged which speak of her unhappiness in the relationship. He said Reeva had struggled with the attention that came with dating him, but that they had been making future plans together. What rubbish. Reeva was already a public figure: a model, a TV presenter, a reality TV personality. She wanted attention – in order for her voice to be heard. Her whole ambition in life was to find a platform so that she could have a voice for the causes she cared about. If Joe Bloggs stands up, no one is going to listen, but Reeva always said, If you're known, you have a voice. That was her plan. To say she struggled with attention was nonsense.

Then the worst bit. I still have nightmares about thinking of her behind the locked toilet door unable to summon help. Here was Oscar, sobbing, describing how he held her body in his arms once he had smashed through the door with his cricket bat. He said he saw the key, took it and unlocked the door, flung it open and sat over Reeva crying. 'I don't know how long I was there for,' he said. 'She wasn't breathing.'

I couldn't wait to leave the court after that. It was a terrible night for me, going back to the guest house with that image in my head, and then returning the next morning to hear him continue to give his version of what happened just after he shot Reeva. It was hard to sit there, day in, day out, hearing all the tiny details and all the time to be thinking my baby must have been so scared. That's what kills me to this day. I had to strain to hear his words through the sobs and sniffles, but he said he had carried her down the stairs and tried to help her breathe and stop the bleeding. 'Reeva had already died while I was holding her, before the ambulance arrived so I knew there was nothing more I could do for her,' he said. And that was how my daughter's life ended.

Gerrie Nel began his cross-examination. This was the crux of the matter and I knew it would be both the worst and the most important part of the trial to sit through. Would Oscar stick to his version? Gerrie's aim was to try to make him break down and tell the truth, but even before the cross-examination process people had commented about how hard it would be to make Oscar crack. He was a world-class athlete, a winner, they argued. He was self-centred and arrogant, but more relevantly he knew how to get in a zone, put on his sportsman's blinkers and focus purely on getting himself to a given finish line without distraction. His goal in this case was not to deviate from the version of events he had given in order to leave the judge thinking it could reasonably possibly be true.

Gerrie began in feisty form. The court was shown the so-called 'zombie stopper' video of Pistorius at a shooting range using the same Black Talon bullets he fired into Reeva. This was shown, despite Barry Roux's objections. Oscar had said he didn't even know what a zombie stopper was and here was a video showing the contrary. It was horrendous, seeing how trigger-happy he was, firing these bullets into a watermelon and laughing at the mess they made on impact. It was Gerrie's attempt to make Oscar take responsibility for ending Reeva's life. He made him look at photos of her bloodied head and said, 'You saw how the bullet made the watermelon explode. You know that the same thing happened to Reeva's head.' There were gasps all around the court. I almost forgot to take a breath and appreciated the squeezes on my arm from those sitting on either side of me. Look. Have a look, Gerrie insisted. Take responsibility. What did you do? You killed Reeva, that's what you did. And still Oscar said he had just made a mistake. He was crying and sobbing . . . That was the moment I thought he was going to break down and confess. But he never did. And that was a disappointment, because if he had said, 'This is what happened . . . and I am so sorry . . .' and asked for mercy from everyone who loved Reeva, people might actually have respected him.

Thereafter Nel was out to highlight the numerous inconsistencies in Oscar's bail hearing and his testimony, such as whether or not he went out onto the balcony before the shooting. He forced Oscar to admit that he had reconstructed some of his evidence. Oh my word Gerrie was tenacious. I felt positive that we seemed to be inching towards some truth when Gerrie informed Oscar, 'We will have to test what you reconstructed and what you remember.'

To be honest, the level of detail and nuance was too much for me. I'm not a pedantic person by nature; I go on instinct. Over the next few days I listened and watched as Oscar was vague, evasive and shifty by turn. He'd say, I don't remember. I don't know. Sometimes he'd even blame his legal team as he resisted Gerrie's attempts to dismantle his version of events. Nothing added up to a coherent picture. He insisted he did not intend to kill anyone, let alone Reeva. He said pulling the trigger was 'an accident'. What? Four times an accident? He admitted that 'objectively' there was no reason to shoot on that night. Asked why he didn't just fire a warning shot into the bathroom, he replied 'because the bullet may have ricocheted and hit me'. He had time to think that through, then. As Gerrie said, 'It's all about you. It's me, myself and I.' And that was so true. When he was asked why it took him so long to answer the question, he said 'Because my life is on the line here.'

No matter how he squirmed, Gerrie reminded him that he believed Oscar's version of events was 'a lie' and that he would argue Reeva 'ran screaming' from an argument with him. He questioned him about his attitude to security and forced Oscar to admit that he wasn't concerned about a balcony window that had been left open. I could not help but recall Oscar wasn't concerned about leaving Reeva alone to house-sit this very same house while he went away for days at a time over Christmas and New Year. He pressed him on why, if he had heard a noise, he had not then asked Reeva if she had heard a noise, too. And why he had not waited for her to respond. He asked why he had moved towards the danger when he heard a noise, rather than go to Reeva in the bedroom. He pointed out that Oscar was changing his defence between saying he thought he was under attack to saying it was an accident. He said Reeva did not scream, but she would definitely have screamed. I know my daughter and she was very vocal. We just hoped the judge would see through his version. We clung to the fact that Judge Masipa is known to be very thorough, very fair.

I lost count of the temporary adjournments the judge allowed for Oscar to recover his composure. He was crying and sobbing, puking into his green bucket, hysterical. Gerrie slowed down a bit. He did not want to be a bully. He got the message that he could only go so far. He wanted to show the pictures of Reeva again but decided against it, because it would be too much for Oscar, and then the judge would have sympathy for Oscar.

When they went through the injuries and stuff, maybe he did feel sick about what he'd done. Apparently he has an anxiety condition where he vomits when he's emotional. To look at him now, he's a pathetic figure. He looks as if his insides are shrivelled up. He looks haunted. He's already been punished in a way. You can never get away from your head, you know. Whatever is in his head is in his head forever. He will have to live with that.

Gerrie ended his five-day cross-examination with a stark summary of what we all believe happened. 'You fired four shots through the door whilst knowing that she was standing behind the door . . . She was locked into the bathroom and you armed yourself with the sole purpose of shooting and killing her.'

'That is not true,' Oscar maintained.

After seeing the protagonist centre stage, it was back to the bit-part players in the drama: the witnesses called by the defence. Roger Dixon testified on more forensic debates, ballistics evidence, the depth of darkness in the bedroom, the comparative sounds of a cricket bat hitting wood and a gun being fired. Gerrie Nel grilled Dixon, asserting the fact that he was trained as a geologist and had not been part of the police forensics department for several years. When we adjourned for coffee, Jennifer and I could hear the detectives laughing in their room next door. They thought Gerrie had annihilated that Dixon guy. The prosecuting team updated me constantly. They told me what was going on and told me not to worry because they had lots up their sleeve.

We needed those breaks for coffee, lunch and tea. The formality of sitting in a court is exhausting You need to let off steam and stretch your legs. It becomes very uncomfortable sitting for hours on the hard bench. You sit in the same position. One of your legs goes dead so you cross them the other way, and back again, and then sit up a little bit straighter to let another side of your bottom take the strain. I was grateful Barry was watching on the couch at home. He could never sit like that. All that detail. All that nit-picking. That verbal war of attrition between the legal teams. I just tried to keep my shoulders up straight and show dignity. The press referred to me as Stoneface, but a lot of people said they admired my composure. I didn't say anything. I didn't give anything away. I listened to every word. I was told that, when this was over, I might be able to say something to him. They may give me a chance to speak to him in the event of a sentencing. They may. I didn't know. What unsettled me was the way he seemed so protected. He has had special treatment, but he is not vulnerable. It was Reeva's bad luck that she met him, because sooner or later he would have killed someone. I do believe that. The previous girlfriend, Samantha Taylor, had the gun waved in her face a few times. She was only seventeen and she said he threw tantrums and dictated to her and she was probably so young that she just took it. But Reeva was a woman who would stand her own ground.

On the final day before the trial adjourned for a two-week break over Easter, Judge Thokozile Masipa reprimanded the 'unruly' behaviour in the overflow room adjacent to the main courtroom where more media follow the proceedings via a giant TV screen. I was petrified of the judge, she was a real stickler. If you came in late, you had to stand by the door and bow to her. If a cellphone went off, she would turn to the culprit and say, '*What* is going on over there?' I didn't just switch my phone off, I took it to pieces. The battery was out. One day I woke up with a tickly cough and stayed at the guest house because I wouldn't have dared cough in court. One of the detectives' phones went off and he went various shades of red and purple like a naughty schoolboy and didn't know where to look. She said to him, 'You will leave the court immediately. I'm not listening to this.' One of the ANC ladies phones went off with a ringtone that sounded like a car firing up and I was so glad I wasn't her! Another day she had to give a lecture forbidding eating and drinking in court and asking members of the press to stop jumping over the benches. There must be respect for the court, she said.

*

The Trial

The trial resumed after Easter with yet more witnesses called by the defence. I understood this is how the criminal justice system works: that the accused is presumed innocent until proven guilty and does not have to prove his innocence. I realised all the defence had to do was to argue a version of events that fitted the forensic evidence while the onus was on the state to prove guilt beyond a reasonable doubt. But what I also saw was that this would be a very hard thing to do when there were only two people present: Reeva, who was dead, and Oscar, who had admitting shooting her, and who now, by his own admission, was trying to save his own life. He knew his entire future was in the balance.

So I sat through witnesses who expanded on Oscar's alleged distress after the incident. We heard Johan Stander, a neighbour, recall receiving a phone call from Oscar asking him to 'Please, please, please, come to my house, I shot Reeva, I thought she was a burglar.' The neighbour's daughter, Carice Viljoen, said he was desperately asking for an ambulance as he held her body, 'praying to God the whole time to save her life. He just kept on begging Reeva to just stay with him and not leave him. He was begging and pleading with Reeva to please stay with him. He was saying "stay with me, my love, stay with me".' She said that when Oscar went to get Reeva's bag to prove ID for the paramedics, she feared he would get the gun from the bathroom and shoot himself, so she ran after him. Another neighbour, Michael Nhlengethwa, said he heard a man crying in a high-pitched voice with the words: 'No, please, please, no.' But how did he know for sure the 'high-pitched voice' was a man? The defence challenged the prosecution on the time Reeva would have last eaten, the position she was in behind the door when the bullet struck her arm and the rate of gunshots. A ballistics expert said he believed that four shots were fired in quick succession, supporting Oscar's claim that he shot quickly in a state of panic. If that was the case, how did one miss her?

I felt very uncomfortable when a social worker and probation officer was called to the stand to say that, because the media had been reporting he had been feigning grief, she wanted to testify that Oscar seemed 'a heartbroken man' when she met him the day after the shooting. In my view, he may well have been crying, but who was he crying for? He could have been crying for himself and for the end of his life as he had known it. Then a psychiatrist, Dr Merryll Vorster, advanced her belief that he had an anxiety disorder that stemmed from his double amputation at an early age. She said: 'Individuals with an anxiety disorder work hard to control their environment and be very prepared in order to alleviate their levels of anxiety.'

Gerrie Nel was quick to challenge her assessment, pointing out his lack of concern over a broken window and the fact that ladders, which could have allowed someone to enter his home, had been left unattended. But, with his mental state under question, Oscar's defence team could claim diminished responsibility and so the prosecution asked that he undergo a psychiatric examination. Judge Masipa agreed: 'It is necessary to emphasise that an application of this nature is never taken lightly, as it is an integral part of a fair trial, having regard to the above, I am satisfied . . . and I shall grant that order.' And so, he was ordered to undergo a month of psychiatric observation at Weskoppies psychiatric hospital. In another concession that seemed to be unnecessarily lenient towards him, he was allowed to be an outpatient at the hospital for thirty days. He would be monitored seven hours a day, five days a week. He didn't have to make the trip at the weekends or overnight – even though the moment his alleged anxiety issues caused him to shoot a gun came in the small hours of the night.

Another long break gave people more time to talk and analyse and offer their views. Each day in court was being televised with a further highlights package in the evening. The trial was coming into peoples' sitting rooms and everyone had an opinion or a theory. People told me they'd heard Oscar had been coached to act distressed on the witness stand, that he'd even had acting lessons. Others informed me that all athletes know how to empty their stomachs before a big race and that

223

was why he was able to retch and vomit so dramatically in court as if in grief. Others said he had a condition which meant he vomited whenever he became emotional. What was a Chinese Whisper or a rumour or a fact, I didn't know, but the impression I got was that no one in the world beyond the courtroom bought into his version of events. They believed he'd hired the best legal team money could buy to back up a story that fitted around the forensic evidence.

If the defence had hopes that the psychiatric evaluation would assist its case, we were pleased to hear they were quashed when the report compiled by four mental health experts was sent back with a resounding and unanimous conclusion that Oscar Pistorius was perfectly sane when he shot Reeva. Gerrie Nel recited the findings into the court record: 'Mr Pistorius did not suffer from a mental defect or a mental illness at the time of the commission of the offence that would have rendered him criminally not responsible for the offences charged ... Mr Pistorius was capable of appreciating the wrongfulness of his act and of acting in accordance of an appreciation of the wrongfulness of his act.' It seemed to me that Team Pistorius had introduced the argument to detract attention from Oscar's dismal performance on the witness stand in an attempt to restore his credibility. But it had backfired. The defence now had a few last witnesses to call – including the surgeon who had amputated his legs as a child.

The Trial

That same day, the judge examined Oscar's stumps at close range. He was asked to remove his prosthetics and walk in the court to assess the mobility he has on his stumps. He looked so tiny, you know. It did prompt sympathy for him from everyone present. I felt sorry for him actually. I can't believe I went through that emotion, considering he took my daughter from me, but I'm not a cruel person, I don't want revenge. If he walks free, he walks free. If he goes to jail for a couple of years, what's the difference? It's not going to change my life. My beautiful girl is never coming back. She's never going to have a baby, never going to get married, never going to have a wedding dress, never going to do all the good in the world that she had set her heart on. And I know that she was ready for all that. She was in the prime of her life. The sky was the limit – and she ends up a spirit in the sky.

Five more days of evidence ushered forward an acoustics expert who questioned whether neighbours 177 metres away could have heard screams coming from the toilet, or identified whether the individual screaming was a man or a woman, with Gerrie Nel arguing that 'more often than not' you could. The defence put up Oscar's long-term manager Peet Van Zyl, to whom he is obviously close. He said a measure of the strength of the relationship was that Reeva was the first girlfriend Oscar ever asked to accompany him overseas, but the next day Gerrie Nel produced an email showing that in 2012 he had received passport details so that Oscar's previous girl-friend Samantha Taylor could accompany him overseas. We also heard a professor talk about the challenges faced by disabled people generally, and athletes especially. These witnesses made me wriggle. Throughout the case, the judge had allowed so much discussion of him and his emotions because he has no legs and therefore can claim a vulnerability, but this is a man who became a sporting hero precisely because he does not consider himself 'disabled'. He had proved he could compete against able-bodied athletes at world-class level. That requires the opposite of vulnerability; it requires phenomenal mental strength. There was nothing fragile about him. Besides, a lot of people have mobility problems.

We were nearing the conclusion of the first phase of the case now, and it was a day of dramatic talk and whispers outside the court. Luckily I didn't see it but we heard an Australian television channel had aired footage of Oscar re-enacting the night he shot and killed Reeva. It wasn't mentioned directly in court but both legal terms discussed it in private. Surely it undermined Barry Roux's argument that Oscar could not have carried out the shooting on his stumps because of limited ability? It seemed he was much more stable and mobile on his stumps than had been argued by his defence lawyers in court. Wayne Derman, a professor in disability sports, insisted that running on stumps was difficult for him.

Gerrie Nel asked him up front if he had considered that the accused might have been lying? 'Of course I have,' he replied.

At last the defence rested its case. We were not due back in court until 7 and 8 August for closing arguments.

6 August 2014

A month later it was time to leave the running of the Barking Spider to the team again and hand care of the dogs and cat over to Simone. For the first time, Barry was considered well enough to travel and attend court. Together, we would fly to Pretoria and take up position on the family bench of courtroom GD to hear the closing arguments of the respective legal teams. It killed Barry that he couldn't be in court every day. He set out to watch every minute on TV, but walked away whenever it got too much for him. For a very long time he couldn't even say Reeva's name. To this day, it just wells up in him. We all handle our grief the way we can ... We travelled with Dup, Truia and Tania Koen (Dup's instructing attorney and Jennifer's stepdaughter) and met up with Kim and other friends and family members in the High Court. Dup had explained that over two days we would hear Gerrie Nel, for the state, ask the judge to reject Oscar's version of events and then it would be the turn of Barry Roux, for the defence, to wrap up their case, where they would try to argue that Oscar's exaggerated response to the fear of an intruder was due to his vulnerability as a double amputee. The verdict would hinge on whether Judge Masipa believed the accused's version of events. I warned Barry that the ordeal in sitting through a concentrated recap of thirty-nine days of court proceedings would be an intense emotional seesaw – hearing 'our side' on one day against Oscar's on the next. We could bear sitting through the prosecution case, painful as it was, because it was the story we in our heart of hearts believed to be true; listening to a day of the defence would make our blood boil.

We had our armoury of little pills to help keep stress at bay. I was still worried about the impact on Barry of his first sighting of Oscar, but I was comforted to have him by my side. The one positive outcome of the trial has been that this whole gruelling experience has transformed our relationship. We were separated for fourteen years, which is a long time not to live under the same roof with someone, and it was a difficult transition after I'd returned to him. We've been in contact every day of our lives since our marriage in 1981. I never went out with anyone else. I wasn't interested. It's Barry I've always loved. We always had money worries and that was stressful and draining. It was a horrible thing. People would phone me because Barry would say, here's my wife's number, she organises everything. And I got tired of that. I do love him. He is a lovely person. Everyone loves Barry. And now we've become much closer again. In our grief, at first he'd pick on me or I'd pick on him, and that was hurtful to both of us when we only had each other to lean on. It became a habit. Many marriages do not survive this sort of tragedy, but Barry came to me one morning during this extended trial process and said he realised he hadn't always been the best husband in the world but that I was going to see a different person from now on. He was going to be the husband I deserved. That was a big thing for me. Maybe what I've always wanted. And he's so sweet, you know. He's so considerate. He'll make me a cup of tea in the morning and he'll do helpful things. He's like a different person.

During this recent adjournment, we heard reports that Oscar had been involved in an incident with a man in a nightclub, where he was allegedly drunk, unruly and boasting about the power of his family's wealth. Yet another statement from the efficient Pistorius family PR machine claimed otherwise, stating he had been aggressively interrogated by a fellow club goer. The statement also dwelt on his 'loneliness and alienation'. As Barry and I agreed, it is a sad situation all round. Here is a man who once had status and now everyone feels sorry for him. He cut a pathetic figure. And we have lost our beautiful daughter.

We arrived and found the media excited by the presence of the two fathers: Barry and Henke Pistorius, the father from whom Oscar was estranged and who was making his first appearance in court since 3 March. It emphasised just how high the stakes were at this crucial stage of the trial.

Gerrie Ncl began with a quote from *Rumpole of the Bailey*. 'With all due respect to your ladyship,' he said, 'I was thinking a criminal trial is a very blunt instrument for digging out the truth.' He said this was a case where they had had to work very hard – but they would get to the truth. As he put the case to the judge, he maintained Oscar was guilty of murder. He argued that the accused's actions in fetching the gun and walking down the corridor towards the bathroom indicates premeditation. Oscar had plenty of alternative courses of action if he truly feared an intruder: 'He had lots of time for reflection. He made up his mind in the bedroom when he armed himself. That is pre-planning.'

He described him as an 'appalling witness' whose testimony was 'devoid of truth' and said he was 'more interested in fending for his life than in entrusting the court with a truthful account.' He went through a baker's dozen of significant incongruities in the defence case, arguing that conflicting evidence about the position of fans and a duvet in his bedroom proved Oscar was tailoring his evidence to mask the fact that he knew it was Reeva in the bathroom when he fired through the locked toilet door. He maintained that there was no proof that the police tampered with the crime scene and that the position of items in the bedroom meant the defence version cannot be true. He told the judge that whether he believed the person behind the door was an intruder or Reeva, it was murder by *dolus directus* (premeditated murder) or *dolus eventualis* (when he must have known he was likely to kill the person by firing). He summed up: 'The accused intended to kill a human being. He knew there was a human being in that toilet. That's his evidence. He is guilty of murder. There must be consequences for it.'

It was painful re-living the scenario yet again as Nel insisted Oscar knowingly fired at Reeva. She was facing the door when he fired directly at her. He said WhatsApp messages between the pair showed the state of the relationship – they were having problems – and they showed Reeva was scared of him. A witness heard an argument; another saw the bathroom light on. Her stomach contents indicated she was awake and eating hours after he claimed they had gone to sleep. 'Nobody went to bed in that house,' he said. 'Nobody was sleeping.' He concluded by arguing that the three other charges revealed a pattern of behaviour in which the accused acts recklessly and does not take responsibility for his actions.

It was a very intense day, but the next day was worse, unspeakably worse. Even though I watched the proceedings with Tania on a screen in another room rather than remaining in court, it was very discomfiting to sit through the arguments formulated to 'save' the accused. Barry Roux said the trial should have begun with a charge of culpable homicide rather than murder, but insisted that Oscar in any case should be acquitted. His argument was that if the firing of the gun was purely reflexive, he lacked criminal capacity. If there was a thought process, it was 'putative private defence' (self-defence) because he believed he was in danger – he believed an intruder was coming out of the toilet. He had no motive to kill Reeva.

Harsh intakes of breath were heard when Barry Roux compared Oscar's years of disability to an abused woman who kills her husband after many assaults. Was he playing to Judge Masipa's well-known antipathy to men who abuse their partners? It was a strange comparison to make, but he used it to maintain that the shooting was a reflexive action after a 'slow burn' of vulnerabilities led to a point at which he had 'had enough'. He was anxious and acting on 'primal instinct'.

Roux then presented the judge with a timeline to counter the state's version of events – particularly that the fatal shots were fired at 3.17 a.m., not 3.12 a.m. He said noises heard at 3.17 a.m. were the thuds of the cricket bat as Pistorius broke down the toilet door. He states that the shots were earlier, and that the screams heard before 3.17 a.m. came from Oscar, not Reeva, who he argued was already fatally wounded. He also said it was 'fatal for the state' that a security guard went past the house at 2.20 a.m. and heard no arguing.

It was horrible to hear the defence pull to bits the version of events we believed to be true. He dismissed the neighbours' accounts, alleging contradictions in several testimonies regarding the number of screams and gunshots heard. He also produced photographs that showed an officer touching items in the bedroom to allege that police had disturbed the scene. He ended, surprisingly, by saying his client should be found guilty of a separate charge of negligently discharging a firearm in a restaurant, but insisted he did not deliberately pull the trigger. He 'made a mistake'.

And with that, we were back to Port Elizabeth again for almost five weeks as Judge Thokozile Masipa was expected to deliver a verdict on 11 September.

19 August 2014

I woke up with a heavy heart. Reeva would have been thirty-one today. We would have been phoning her, talking to her about her plans to celebrate. Perhaps she would even have been with us, visiting Port Elizabeth. She was twenty-nine when she died. We have missed celebrating her thirtieth birthday and she wasn't here to mark Barry's seventieth in 2013 – two milestones which should have been happy family occasions. Life goes on, but with such emptiness.

On this August day, we decided to go early down to the beach in Summerstrand, to the exact spot where we had scattered her ashes and released doves and had the minister pray for her soul in the presence of the family and precious friends. So we went, Barry and I alone. We took beautiful pink roses and we waded into the water and sent them out to the sea for her and the dolphins. We said Happy Birthday and felt very sad, missing her lots and lots. It seems to get worse, not better. How are we supposed to live happily without her? It's too much really. It's like a constant pain in the chest. We miss her so much. She was such a wonderful person, kind and loving and always devoted to us. It's hard to live without her. Time is not the healer people promise. Each day that passes just extends the time since we last saw her or heard her on the phone or wondered how she was. The passing of time makes us miss her more. She was so *full of life*.

We remained lost in our thoughts on the beach. It was about 10 a.m. and Wayne, her first love, arrived on the beach to wish her Happy Birthday too. He had brought a bottle of champagne and carried an assortment of flowers. We greeted him warmly. He's like an adopted son to us, you know. After sending his flowers out to sea for her, too, Wayne poured Barry and himself a glass of champagne and poured the rest into the sea for Reeva.

Happy birthday my dearest, darling daughter.

The Verdict

Thursday 11 September 2014. The date loomed as the culmination of everything. We could hardly believe that our nightmare had begun 574 days ago – and we were still looking for answers as to what happened to our beautiful daughter on Valentine's Day 2013. Today was the day we expected to get them. We needed the truth. We wanted justice for Reeva. Was that too much to ask?

Judge Masipa's verdict was predicted to be long and detailed and delivered over two days. The judge is known for being thorough and she had to sift through evidence and testimonies from thirty-seven witnesses who gave evidence for the state and for the defence. She would have to give reasons why the court had accepted their evidence or not, and whether or not the burden of truth had been discharged by the state, 'on whom the onus rested'. We were to hear that phrase a lot over the next two days. It became quite ominous. As South Africa does not have trials by jury, the verdict was that of the judge and the two assessors. It wasn't clear at what point on Thursday or Friday she would announce her verdict on Count 1, the only charge we were interested in. We could only sit and wait.

As a family, we had been very tense leading up to this reconvening of the court. None of us could say we were in a good place. For me, it wasn't just the gnawing emotional heaviness and the fidgety feeling of anticipation. Physically, I felt terrible too. I'm not a heavy drinker, but I had decided to give up my evening glass of wine for a month because I wanted to be clear-headed and fully alert on the day we heard the verdict. I did not want to miss a nuance of the ruling. However, I felt awful throughout my abstinence – where was that bounce and energy I'd expected from a detox? – but I'd made a pact with God not to have even a sip until 11 September, and I'd been holding out. In addition, Barry and I had mixed feelings and expectations about reaching this stage. We'd been warned that the period after a trial, no matter what the outcome, is the worst phase of bereavement for the family of a victim of crime. We had suspended our grief in order to channel our focus into seeing justice done for Reeva in the court, and then . . . what? It would be time to come home, sit back and work through our grief, and face up to the reality that she was never coming back. We would have to try to start life afresh again. How on earth we would do that we couldn't imagine.

Spelling out a finality, the delivery of the verdict was another grim reminder that we had lost Reeva for ever; it was another prompt to trigger a tidal wave of grief. But there was comfort in numbers as we set off from the guest house in two vehicles – Barry, Jennifer, Dup, Truia, Tania, Michael, Lyn, Kim, Dion and I – braced to walk through the media frenzy. I had never seen so many camera crews, reporters and photographers in my life. They weren't just thronging the pavements and crowding the walkway as usual. This time photographers were perched on boxes and step ladders to claim a better vantage point; reporters talked live to cameras announcing our arrival as we approached. Walking through that circus was a bombardment of flashing lights, clicking noises and murmuring voices. This was, after all, the day the world expected to hear the verdict in South Africa's 'Trial of the Century'. I didn't have any tactics for dealing with this attention. You just have to look where you're going. 'How are you today, June?' 'June, how are you feeling?' I understood everyone wanted to know my opinion. I was so close to the story they somehow thought I exuded some clues about what was going to happen.

Once inside and through security – the irony of being frisked for a firearm was never lost on me – we filed in to our horribly familiar bench in the empty courtroom. A pretty third-year law student presented me with a bouquet of red roses tied with a pink ribbon – a lovely gesture. Eleven roses to mark the date, she said. 'Oscar is always getting letters, balloons and teddy bears,' she said. 'And this is all about Reeva.'

Returning yet again to courtroom GD was like a re-run of the start of the trial and of the opening of the Heads of Arguments. The Myers family arrived – the two sisters Gina and Kim and their mother forming a row of raven-haired women in the row behind us. They were followed by Reeva's friends Darren Fresco and his wife Beatrix, and Kristin Ellis looking elegant in glasses and a black dress. The Pistorius family filled up their side of our shared front bench: Uncle Arnold and his wife Lois, Oscar's father Henke, his sister Aimee, various cousins. We waited in a strange atmosphere of tension cut by the chatty sounds of the regular attendees greeting each other. Through a tragic incident we've had familiarity forced on us – the friends and family of Reeva and Oscar, the respective legal teams, the international press correspondents and public gallery supporters. We're all linked for life by this legal process.

Carl Pistorius, Oscar's older brother, was wheeled up to the front of the court in his wheelchair, still recovering from the serious injuries he had suffered in a high-speed head-on car smash on 1 August. His family must have been suffering with him in intensive care on top of Oscar's plight. Even while they'd attended Closing Arguments, Carl was in ICU being treated for multiple fractures and internal lacerations to vital organs. And this was six years after he had been involved in a road accident where a female motorcyclist died after colliding with his vehicle; he was later acquitted for culpable homicide for the woman's death. On the dot of nine o'clock Oscar walked in, nodded to us, and marched over to greet Carl who was in a smart grey suit with both legs fully extended in front of him in bulky white plastic medical boots. Barry Roux wrapped Oscar in a hug, and the court awaited.

'This is awesome,' I heard someone say. 'This is history in the making. This is HUGE.'

Shortly before 9.30 a.m., the judge's registrar, accompanied by two heavily armed tactical task team members, entered the court and placed the written judgement on the bench. The armed security officers positioned themselves on either side of the bench. Hush descended as we were called to be upstanding for the judge. At 9.34 a.m., she arrived, a small and weary figure in her red gown, limping up the few steps to her bench. We all did the bowing business, and then without delay she picked up the papers that lay on the desk in front of her: the papers that contained the verdict known only to herself and her two assessors. The 73-page ruling had been typed up in secret and kept under lock and key until this moment . . .

Deep breaths all around. A few nervous coughs. The shuffling of paper. Muttered prayers along the Pistorius bench.

Judge Masipa began by setting out an overview of the case, talking us through the layout of the crime scene and the circumstances under which the couple were there together. She spoke very softly in a calm, measured tone. Everyone in court leant forward and strained to catch her all-important words. Initially they amounted to a distillation of the basic facts. She went through the charges and the accused's not guilty pleas to Counts 1, 2, 3 and 4. To me, it was a cloud of legalese: provisions, sections, schedules, acts, contraventions, alternative counts and so on, and I patiently waited for the first comment that would indicate where she was heading with her judgement. She named the members of the defence and prosecution teams, and repeated the accused's 'explanation of plea' that Count 1 was a tragic incident after he mistakenly believed intruders had entered his house. Here, it struck me freshly again, how unbelievable Oscar's story was – I mean, how can he have talked to Reeva in bed beside him as he got out of bed to move the fans as he described, and then not renew a conversation when he then immediately thought he heard intruders in the bathroom and bent down to get his gun from under the bed and walk towards the bathroom? It just didn't make sense.

Meanwhile, the judge had continued reading from her papers, stating that the accused gave no explanation for Counts 2, 3 and 4. She summarised the prosecution case and went on to note witnesses who heard 'a woman engaged in an argument', 'screams interpreted as a woman in distress' and 'sounds of gunshots and a man shouting for help'. At last, we were moving towards the crux of the matter.

But still Judge Masipa was setting out the foundations of the case. She moved on to the 'common cause facts', i.e. those that are not disputed by either side: that on 14 February 2013, shortly after three in the morning, screams were heard from the accused's house; that the accused, while on his stumps, fired four shots at the toilet door; that at the time the shots were fired the deceased was inside the toilet; that the door of the toilet was locked from the inside; that the door of the toilet opened to the outside, that is into the bathroom; that three of the four shots struck the deceased; that the deceased sustained a wound on the right thigh, a wound on the left upper arm, a head injury and a wound on the web of the fingers and that the deceased died from multiple gunshot wounds. She added further 'common cause' facts: that soon after the shots had been fired the accused called for help; that he used a cricket bat to break down the door; that he removed the deceased from the toilet to the hallway down-stairs; that he was very emotional soon after the incident and that he was seen trying to resuscitate the deceased. She con-cluded that the issues were limited to whether at the time the accused shot and killed 'the deceased' he had the requisite intention, and if so, whether there was any premeditation.

The deceased. I recoiled at every mention of the word. I mean, that was my daughter. Reeva.

I thought the formal introduction to the ruling was going to go on forever, but suddenly the judge indicated she had chiselled days and days of testimony from multiple witnesses aside. She said that issues about whether or not the police contaminated the scene, about the length of an extension cord that had gone missing from the bedroom and the authenticity of photographs of items depicted in various exhibits had paled in significance when one has regard to the rest of the evidence. She reiterated the fact that there were no eye witnesses, but lots of witnesses who testified about what they had heard: gunshots, screams, a woman in distress. She said these had to be discussed together because they were inextricably linked.

And then my heart dropped. Did I detect the first sign that the state's case was found wanting? I could hardly believe it when I heard her pronounce that the evidence of Burger and Johnson must be rejected in its entirety – not because they colluded as the defence argued, but because they were genuinely mistaken owing to the distance. This was devastating. It was Michelle Burger who was so certain she had heard the 'blood-curdling screams'. The judge continued also to dismiss the defence claims that Oscar sounded like a woman when he screamed, decreeing that the identification and interpretation of sounds is tricky when the witnesses have no model or prior experience to compare with. Not even former girlfriend Samantha Taylor, she said, could claim to have heard the accused scream in a life-threatening situation.

I was getting some measure of how the judge filtered evidence for facts that would stick in her opinion. Each piece of evidence had been poured through the mesh of her assessor's sieve. From the outset I understood she could only assess the facts in front of her and she had to go by the letter of the law. We all knew what we believed happened that night, and I just hoped she had enough evidence in front of her. Judge Masipa continued by outlining Reeva's horrendous injuries and the view that bullet damage had rendered her immediately unconscious and unable to scream. The screaming, she proposed, must have come from Oscar. I didn't understand where she had evidence that the four shots were fired in quick succession. If they were shot in rapid succession, how did one miss her? Others were clearly filled with similar dismay. Little did I know that the reporters in the benches behind, interpreting the ruling for their media houses with minute-by-minute updates, were filling Twitter feeds with lines such as: 'She is swerving verdict in favour of OP.'

I concentrated hard. The judge had after all referred to the 'difficult terrain that this court had to traverse to arrive at its conclusion'. She referred to evidence in the form of technology, such as phone records, being 'more reliable than human perception and memory' and then – another blow – asserted that the state had done nothing to undermine the timeline presented by the defence.

What that meant was that she had ruled that the gunshots were fired at 3.12 to 3.14 a.m. and that the noises heard at 3.17 a.m. – which the state alleged were the gunshots – were in fact the bangs of the cricket bat on the wooden toilet door. On that bombshell, the court adjourned for a break.

I glanced towards Oscar. He had slumped forward, alone in his thoughts. No one tried to talk to him. All around me people were shaking their heads, confused. Everything she had been saying suggested she was leaning towards Oscar Pistorius's version of events.

Court resumed. The momentum was definitely going in Oscar's direction. About the defence witnesses who heard a man crying, Judge Masipa said this had the 'ring of truth'. She said Reeva could have had her mobile phone in the toilet for a number of reasons, for example to light the way to the toilet because the light in the toilet cubicle didn't work, but to pick a reason was 'to delve into the realm of speculation'. I was absolutely stunned when she dismissed the WhatsApp messages as proving nothing, declaring that 'normal relationships are dynamic and unpredictable sometimes'. Really? Reeva had said he picked on her 'incessantly'. Do normal relationships allow for a partner to be scared of the other? Scared of the way they snap? In those SMSs he was so very critical of her and derogatory, and it had actually hurt me to realise that he could have treated her like that. At the time of cross-examination, people asked me why Gerrie Nel had not put Oscar on the spot: what happens when you snap? Did you reply to this message? Why not? It was too late to regret missed opportunities. Instead the judge accepted the defence's argument that the majority of messages were loving – but you can't say this was a dreamy, blissful relationship. They had only known each other for three months and we all knew it had been problematic or 'intense', as several of her friends euphemistically remarked on TV documentaries.

The judge went on. She determined the stomach content evidence did not 'help the state case' and noted that a security guard, passing the house at 2.20 a.m., heard no argument. None of this was sitting well with me. My heart dropped.

Her report then switched to an assessment of the defence case. It was an accident. He never intended to kill anyone. He did not purposefully fire into the door. He did fire into the door but did not do so deliberately. He did not aim at the door but the gun was pointed at the door. He did not mean to pull the trigger but did so in fright. He did not have time to think before firing. He believed someone was coming out of the cubicle to attack him. By this stage they were just words going around my head – Oscar's evasive words, contradictory words, desperate words – but I sat up when I heard the judge emphasise one line of her findings. She said that his explanation that 'if he had wanted to kill the intruder, he would have fired higher' was 'inconsistent with someone who shot without thinking'.

The court stood up for another break. It was up, down, up, down, a cliffhanger at every adjournment. But was the momentum swinging back to the state's line? It felt like the judge was playing poker. Every time she seemed to going one direction, she'd play another card with a 'however' and move along another route.

Back for the next instalment, she quickly established that psychiatric assessment showed the accused *did* have criminal capacity and moreover that he could not rely on putative self-defence because he had claimed he never intended to shoot anyone. However – and here was another handbrake turn of a 'however' – she said the intention to shoot did not mean an intention to kill. Again she stressed the onus of proof was on the state to establish that beyond reasonable doubt. Everyone nodded vigorously at her description of Oscar as 'a very poor witness' . . . 'evasive' . . . 'more worried about the impact his answers might have than the questions asked' . . . But there was a ripple of collective surprise when she said: 'The conclusion, that because an accused is untruthful he is therefore probably guilty, must be guided against, as a false statement does not always justify the most extreme conclusion. In the present case the deceased was killed under very peculiar circumstances . . .'

And then we heard that these *very* peculiar circumstances, which did not make sense, would unfortunately remain a matter of conjecture. I was lost. Everyone around us was aghast. After six months of attending court we hadn't learnt any more. With that list of peculiar circumstances, I realised that this entire ordeal of a trial had not come close to providing answers to the many unanswered questions, namely – in the judge's own language – why the accused did not ascertain from the deceased when he heard the window open whether she too had heard anything; why he did not ascertain whether the deceased had heard him since he did not get a response from the deceased before making his way to the bathroom; why the deceased, who was in the toilet and only a few metres away from the accused, did not communicate with the accused, or phone the police as requested by the accused. It made no sense that she did not hear him scream 'get out' at the top of his voice when he ordered the intruders to get out. And why would he fire not one, but four shots, before running back to the bedroom to try to find Reeva?

It was only 11.07 on the first morning of the scheduled two days when Judge Masipa said: 'The timelines as set out in the chronology of events tip the scales in favour of the accused's version in general. Viewed in its totality, the evidence failed to establish that the accused had the requisite intention to kill the deceased, let alone with premeditation. I am here talking about direct intention. The state clearly has not proved beyond reasonable doubt that the accused is guilty of premeditated murder. *There are just not enough facts to support such a finding.*'

And on that dramatic note, the court adjourned for another break.

There was a muted response in the courtroom. It was always considered more likely that he would be found guilty on a lesser count of murder, rather than premeditated murder. Was this the way the judge was leaning? Oscar and Aimee were huddled with their legal team, looking fraught and depressed.

The next session brought up lots of legal definitions such as *aberratio ictus* (accidental harm), whereby A shoots B but instead hits C, and *error in persona*, i.e., the shot was intended for the person behind the door, but that person turned out to be different. I lost track of the definitions and illustrations. I was waiting for the conclusion, but my heart sunk when I heard her say of his alleged fear for his life and that of Reeva: 'There is nothing in the evidence to suggest that this belief was not honestly entertained.'

Then the thunderbolt that caused gasps all around me. She said the evidence did not support the state's case that this was *dolus eventualis* (i.e., that he must have known he was likely to kill the person by firing) because he believed she was in the bedroom. She said his account of this has remained consistent since the night of the shooting. It was 'highly improbable the accused would have made this up so quickly'. The question was: 'Did the accused foresee the possibility of the resultant death, yet persisted in his deed reckless whether death ensued or not? In the circumstances of this case the answer has to be no.'

No? What! Lots of people shook their heads. No, in terms of Reeva, perhaps. But yes in terms of someone, surely – the alleged intruder of his own account?

Her voice intoned: 'The accused therefore cannot be found guilty of murder *dolus eventualis.*'

I didn't look towards Oscar but I later saw the television images of him heaving violently with relief, tears streaming down his face.

Another break, this time for lunch, but we had no appetite for our picnic of crackers. It wasn't so much disbelief in our minds, it was disbelief all around. Whispers grew louder that the judge had misapplied the third question in the test for *dolus eventualis*. I'm not familiar with the ins and outs of law, but we and all our supporters started receiving messages suggesting there'd been an error and perhaps the judge would correct it after the break. Law students in the public gallery were passionate about the 'misinterpretation of law'. But the question should have been 'Could he have foreseen there was a living person behind that door and could he have foreseen that if he fired four bullets someone could be killed?' People were talking about how the state can appeal legal errors and speculating that the judge might correct herself after the break. Social media, the radio, live TV, every form of debate was red-hot with outrage. Upstairs in our room, tears flowed. Gerrie Nel looked downcast. The judge could still find Oscar guilty of culpable homicide, a serious charge, but people feared there was a real possibility that he would now be acquitted as she seemed to have accepted his story that he genuinely feared for his life and was acting in self-defence.

I started thinking of her bag that was packed as if ready to leave. That she was shot wearing a sleeveless black top and shorts, clothes for a summer's day, not her night clothes. That she had brought him a wrapped Valentine's Day gift and card and he had nothing for her – she who set such store in occasions. He would have seen her tweet that day – **What do you have up your sleeve for your love tomorrow??? #getexcited #ValentinesDay** – yet he would disappoint her.

And how could anyone believe that he could not have foreseen that his actions, in shooting four Black Talon bullets into a small confined space, could result in the death of any person behind the door? The ANCWL ladies were angry, carrying placards outside the High Court saying, 'If you kill a woman, you are killing a nation'.

The bottom line we had to accept was that the judge had ruled out a murder conviction. I just could not believe that she found credibility in his version of events when none of us – and no one in the world, it seemed – believed his story. She'd said the state had failed to make its case against him and the evidence they'd presented was purely circumstantial. Maybe she just didn't have enough evidence in front of her.

After lunch we filed wearily down the dimly lit stairs and took our places again in court. Gerrie Nel entered and left again with Barry Roux. We were told they'd been called to the judge's chambers. People wondered aloud whether she was about to correct her perceived error in testing *dolus eventualis*. At 1.13 p.m., Judge Masipa re-appeared and resumed reading her report, which went on to consider the question of culpable homicide and negligence. There was yet more sifting through argument and precedent and circumstances and tests based on 'a reasonable person', but I was no longer interested in the minutiae. I sat up when she said 'the explanation of the conduct of the accused is just that: an explanation. It does not excuse the conduct of the accused'. And again when she concluded she was of the view that 'the accused acted too hastily and used excessive force. In the circumstances,' she said, 'it is clear that his conduct was negligent.'

That was it for the day. That was it for our desire to see justice for Reeva. We returned to the guest house devastated. There was obviously so much more to the story and it had not been uncovered. I felt very, very disappointed. Heartsore, actually, and exhausted. We had come through all of this and we had not got the truth. I felt let down by the justice system, but most of all sad, because I wanted the right thing for Reeva. She died a horrible, painful, terrible death, and she suffered. Her boyfriend shot four times through the door. One of the bullets struck her in the upper left arm which meant she had been facing the door, probably pleading with him, not sitting on the toilet. And I couldn't believe, given the circumstances, that they could not effectively discredit his story of a tragic accident. I thought the state of a relationship was the first and the most crucial thing considered in deaths when only two people were at the scene, and one shot the other? But that's the problem: only the two of them were there that night.

We sat down in the garden of the guest house and had a glass of wine – my first in a month, and which I had visualised drinking not with happiness but with a little more satisfaction than I did that hot afternoon of 11 September. We'd had a plan to go out discreetly later with the family to eat in the private room of a local restaurant, so Barry and I went upstairs to rest. But we couldn't rest. Our phones were being bombarded with messages of shock and sympathy and disbelief and outrage from all over the world. I couldn't help but switch on the television coverage. It was so upsetting, seeing these beautiful images of Reeva interspersed with footage of legal experts querying the judge's application of law and of Oscar sobbing in relief in the dock. I couldn't face eating dinner. My distress became uncontainable. I'd always said I'd hold it in until after the trial, and now my emotions were flooding out. I stayed in my room and hoped sleep would come to me. I wasn't sure if I would be prepared to return to court the next day. I was angry.

The next morning dawned – always the worst time of day for me now – and we had to go back, but for what? I wasn't sure until the last moment if I could climb into the car and set off again for the High Court. What a difference a day had made. Yesterday's headlines – 'Oscar's Moment of Truth' –

had changed to 'Oscar's Great Escape', 'Tears of Relief', 'Athlete a very lucky man – lawyer', 'Not guilty of murder? Judge erred' and 'Appeal looms'. The car radio broadcast opinions of a multitude of legal experts. It was amazing how many legal experts had come out of the woodwork. Some stuck to their view that the state must appeal after a mis-application of law while others mused that if Judge Masipa ruled culpable homicide, a sentence would be at her discretion, and she could even impose a suspended sentence, a non-jail sentence or a fine. Feelings were running high. Someone showed me a tweet from a Johannesburg resident:

This case #OscarTrial has lost sight of the real Victim #Reeva Steenkamp, she has become the 'intruder' and #OscarPistorius the Victim. So sad.

So true.

Oscar arrived in court with a bodyguard, looking more relaxed than usual. Judge Masipa limped into court, flanked by armed bodyguards and a heavy police presence. Were they the same contingent as yesterday? Or did she have more protection because of her controversial judgement? She plunged straight into the three firearm charges. It all washed over me. It was more of the same tactical play from the defence. BBC Africa correspondent Andrew Harding tweets: **I have it on**

good authority that #Oscar Pistorius is only pleading not guilty because he says incident happened on different day. He was referring to the discharge of a gun through the sunroof. Well, I thought that Oscar wasn't in court to tell the truth, just wriggle out of charges on technicalities and save his skin. It was a game. The judge muddled up Counts 2 and 3 and the courtroom collectively squirmed on squeaky benches and coughed as she paused for a long time to shuffle her papers. She proceeded to acquit him of one count of discharging a firearm in public, which prompted more muttering from observers. She found that the state had proved beyond reasonable doubt that he was guilty of another count of discharging a firearm in public. She found him not guilty of illegal possession of ammunition.

She was zooming through her ruling now, and we surely had to be getting close to the moment when she asked him to stand up and hear the court's official verdict.

At 10.15 a.m. the nightmare replayed again in my head as she intoned the following:

'In conclusion, I would like to recap on the four counts. In respect of Count 1, the allegation was that the accused and the deceased had an argument. That the deceased ran and locked herself in the toilet and that the accused followed her there, and fired shots at her through the locked door. Three shots struck her and she died as a result. Evidence led by the state in respect of this count was purely circumstantial. It was not strong circumstantial evidence. Moreover the evidence of various witnesses who gave evidence on what they heard, in what sequence and when, proved to be unreliable. The accused denied the allegations. Notwithstanding that he was an unimpressive witness, the accused gave a version which could reasonably possibly be true. In criminal law that is all that is required for an acquittal as the onus to prove the guilt of an accused, beyond reasonable doubt, rests with the state throughout.'

It was explained to me that as the onus rests with the state, an accused person does not have to be believed to be acquitted. Judge Masipa repeated how phone records supported Oscar's story. She said he acted promptly to seek help after he shot Reeva. He prayed to God to save Reeva. He was distraught. She said 'the accused cannot be found guilty of murder, *dolus directus* or *dolus eventualis*, on the basis of his belief and conduct. It cannot be said that he foresaw that either the deceased or anyone else for that matter might be killed when he fired the shots at the toilet door.' She repeated her view that it cannot be said that he did not have a genuine belief that there was an intruder in the house. 'Evidential material before this court show however that the accused acted negligently. The toilet cubicle was small with little room for manoeuvre.

The Verdict

'Mr Pistorius, please stand up. Having regard to the totality of this evidence in this matter, the unanimous decision of this court is the following:

'*Count 1: Murder, read with Section 51(1) of the Criminal Law Amendment Act, 105 of 1997, the accused is found not guilty and is discharged. Instead, he is found guilty of culpable homicide.*'

We all knew it had been coming, but the impact of her words stunned the courtroom. All around me I heard gasps, sobbing, sniffs as people crumpled. It was unbelievable. The judge was still going over the other counts but none of us on the family bench were taking those in. Kim, next to me, was sobbing uncontrollably and I pulled her towards me for comfort. Her mother Lyn had her head on Kim's other shoulder. We were all in pieces. My heart continued to beat but I didn't feel alive. I was numb. I didn't even think to look at him. I didn't want to see him jubilant, though. I was happy for his family because they've been suffering like we have. They have to believe him, he's family.

Yet another adjournment was announced. Truia and I went upstairs to a different room we had been allocated as a retreat along the prosecutors' corridor and I decided not to return to that courtroom again. I didn't want to know if he won extended bail, as his lawyers were now starting to appeal for. So much concern for him! This wasn't about him in my eyes.

It should have been about Reeva. I couldn't take it a minute longer and I wasn't going to pretend I could. From all over the world, people were phoning and texting me, everyone was very upset. The word travesty echoed in peoples' comments. Donald Trump tweeted **No one has been more guilty of murder since OJ**. Sharon Saincic, Chanelle Henning's mother, said, 'This is the wrong message. It shows if you have money in this country you will walk.' Legal forums were abuzz with suggestions that the judge had made a mistake and she hadn't rectified it. Justine Lang from BBC News tweeted:

One wonders if Judge Masipa has any idea of the rampaging legal storm over her decision to drop murder.

I never imagined I could feel more numb and bereft. During the forty-odd days of the trial, I had often sensed Reeva's presence in the courtroom, but not today. I just felt emptiness. I found the way the judge referred to 'the deceased' so cold. I understood her role was that of an assessor of facts and evidence, but we, the victim's family, hadn't found any closure in the legal process. It was so wrong. How could they believe his story? If he was so paranoid about security, why was the broken window not fixed? Why was the alarm not fixed?

Why was he happy to leave Reeva alone twice, for periods stretching over several nights, in the same house over Xmas and New Year?

As Reeva studied law herself, I wonder what she would make of the judgement, my wise and clever daughter. I imagine she would share the view of her great friend Kristin, her fellow law undergraduate, who sat two rows behind me during the verdict. Kristin had prepared herself for a finding of not guilty on premeditation, but she did not agree with the judge's application of the law, particularly when it came to *dolus eventualis*. She was also dumbfounded by some of the conclusions drawn by Judge Masipa and how she outright dismissed a large portion of the state's case. 'I'm very disappointed,' she said to me. 'And scared that he will get off on a suspended sentence for culpable homicide.'

Back at the guest house, Barry and I sat down with family and friends and discussed how we felt. We were extremely disappointed with the verdict and our conversation went round and round over the same points and peculiar circumstances as if trying to purge ourselves of this horrible feeling of disbelief and shock. It was the worst of double whammies – to lose our daughter and then to see her violent death officially deemed an accident. It was never going to sit with us, this outcome, although we didn't yet know what the sentence would be. To be honest

I really didn't care what would happen to Oscar because my daughter was never coming back. He was still living and breathing. She'd gone for ever. I just couldn't get my head around this verdict. A court of law had believed his story and we had never believed his story. We wanted justice for Reeva and we hadn't got it. Barry had said all along that whatever the verdict would be, whatever the sentence, 'it will be what it will be and we must accept that and carry on with our lives'. That was going to be so difficult now when the conclusion to the trial had not matched what was in our hearts. The judge seemed to believe his version because it fitted in with the accepted timeline. Something had been missed. Only Oscar knew what happened.

I knew in my heart there was more to it. So many questions went unanswered. The clothes on the floor in Oscar's house – my daughter would never have gone to bed leaving her clothes on the floor. And who said the bathroom light wasn't working? When he went in to find her, the lights were on, weren't they? If it was a burglar and he had a gun, which they all do, the burglar would be firing his gun, not hiding. 'He' was the intruder, the aggressor; domestic intruders come in with a purpose.

And Oscar was not a good witness, he was emotional. We had to halt the case all the way through for his dramas. I just didn't believe him. I'm telling you, she was standing behind that door, pleading with him. They said the first shot would have been the most painful and she would have been suffering... I have to live with that thought and it's terrible, terrible.

A lot of comments we received focused on the judge's belief Oscar could not have 'faked' his distress so convincingly after the event and that he could not have stuck to the same story about the intruder so consistently. So many people disagreed. Such behaviour is characteristic of crimes of passion. He could have shot Reeva in a moment of rage, and subsequently been overcome with genuine remorse and emotion.

I didn't want to hurt him. I didn't want revenge. I didn't want to see him go to prison for a long time, but I felt extremely unsettled by the court's conclusion. That was very hard to swallow. Judges go by the law. They have to be careful about the person who is charged. She was very restricted in what she could do. She could only assess what she had in front of her and maybe she didn't have enough evidence in front of her. Barry was right: from the very beginning we have never believed his story because all of this could have been prevented. If he thought that there was somebody in his bathroom, down the passage from his bedroom, his balcony windows were open, he could have shouted for help, he could have pressed an alarm, he could have used his phone to call security, he could have taken Reeva by the hand and shepherded her downstairs away from 'the danger'. There were so many things that he could have done – that any reasonable person would have done – to prevent the catastrophe we have to live with.

The media expect me to feel hostility towards Oscar, but I have forgiven him in the Christian sense. I don't want to carry poison in my body about that. You can make yourself ill. I don't want him to suffer, that's not in my heart. We have no feelings towards him, Barry and I, good or ill. We just want the truth and he is the only person who can fill in the missing blanks of what happened that night. He could have stood up and said, I'm sorry, something terrible happened and I killed her. NOT, I'm sorry, I made a mistake and I killed her. He shot four times through a door into a cramped space knowing what the effect of those kind of bullets would be and he must take full responsibility for that. We are talking about bullets that open explosively with barbs as they penetrate bone and tissue and which have since been withdrawn from sale by the manufacturer.

Barry feels slightly differently. Before he can totally forgive Oscar, he wants to sit down and talk. We'd both like to sit down in private and chat with him. I'm sure he'd like to talk to us as well. It hasn't been appropriate until now, but it would get a lot off our chest. What would we say to him? I don't know. I'm still holding everything inside. I just know that if you believe in God, you must forgive. You can't look for someone to blame and carry that burden inside you because you're also going to get sick. I'm not preaching, but for me and my religious beliefs, I have to forgive in order to survive even. Barry had a stroke from carrying that pain. You can't let it destroy you.

The trial phase is over, but we don't have closure. With this verdict, there is never going to be. How can there be? She's not coming back. I was asked what an appropriate sentence would be, but I didn't want to consider that. It won't make my daughter come back. He has to live for the rest of his life with the knowledge of what he he's done inside his heart. He was a man who had status, and now he has pity. He looks haunted. He may have won the court case, but he isn't a winner long-term. He has to live with what he did for ever.

Legacy

The morning after the verdict, I found a feather, a little white one, just in front of where I had put my make-up in the bedroom. 'She's back,' I smiled to myself. If she had been with me in spirit in the courtroom for the verdict she'd have realised the way it was going. Maybe that was why I couldn't sense her on the second day. She decided not to hang around and see us suffer. She wouldn't wish Oscar harm – she believed in karma and what goes around comes around and all that – but she wouldn't have wanted to listen to the judge's conclusion at all. She was not resting in peace.

The feathers lift me so much. I've found them on the balcony at the guest house, on the windowsill in our room at the High Court, and once on the guest-house doorstep as we were leaving for court.

'Ah, here's a feather,' I said.

'And . . . ?' said Tania.

I explained that it was Reeva sending me a sign, at least in my heart that's what I think.

'She's letting me know that she's here with me.'

Well, turn the taps on. Tania was finished by the time we got to court.

'I'm sorry,' she sniffed. 'It's just the thought of it.'

I find feathers in the oddest places at home as well. It's a Reeva and me thing, because of the pact we made years ago. The more I think about it, the more I wonder if she somehow knew she hadn't long to live. She was so busy, you know. She was such a people person. She packed so much in and drew so many people to her. She came, she did her good, and now she's gone: a beautiful soul. As Mrs Ntlangu of St Dominic's Priory suggested so poignantly, 'We in the world want the cream. Maybe God also wants the cream in heaven?' Even as a very young woman, Reeva always spoke as if she'd considered her role in life. I see that now, and not only in her farewell speech on *Tropika* when she mused that it was not just your journey in life but the way that you go out and make your exit that is so important, you can either make a positive or a negative impact. Even back in 2005, when she was a finalist in the *Herald* Miss PE modelling competition, she stood on the stage and said she hoped to show young women in Port Elizabeth, and perhaps South Africa, that while it was important to have a professional ambassadorial role with a career, it was also important to be young and spirited and free.

We must never forget what Reeva stood for. She loved people. She loved everybody; and it was her heart that went out to engage people. She was someone who stood out – in her family, at school, in her career, among her friends – for having an innate way of fitting in, for trying to excel in everything and for appreciating every little blessing in life. It's important for me to hold on even to those tiny everyday things she taught us because they make us smile, like remembering the back section when I do my hair or keeping the fridge orderly.

We are all finding our own way of coping. Abigail told me her fondest memories are of her and Reeva lazing around, drinking tea, painting their nails and talking about their future. She remembers how the girls would be going somewhere and Reeva would say let's stop and smell the roses. 'It's amazing how I do those things now,' Abby said. 'She taught me a lot about stopping to look at the good things in life instead of always being on a mission.' Every day she thinks of Reeva teaching her how to put on mascara because it always puts a smile on her face. (For the record, it involves placing the wand deep into the base of your eyelashes and mushing it left and right before brushing up through the lashes to create length.)

Like most of us, Abby feels no hatred for Oscar. As she sees

it, wherever he goes in this world his life as he knew it is finished, and that's karma in her view. But the circumstances of
Reeva's death trouble her. They were due to Skype each
other on Saturday 16 February and update each other about
what was going on in their lives. As they were both so interested in spirituality and the power of intuition, Abby told me
she decided to seek out a medium in London to see if she
could get some answers. Two weeks before she died, Reeva,
a Leo, had posted on her Twitter account:

**Leos wish they had phones up in heaven, so they
could talk to people they miss.**

Abby researched it very carefully. The person she chose knew
nothing about her. And her experience was quite extraordinary. She told me a spirit guide came through to her who said
she had a young girl, and she's beautiful and she's got long
curly dark hair and she's standing behind a door. The guide
said she's very shy, no, she's not shy, she's a bit sheepish, almost
like you might not want to speak to her. Okay, she's saying
sorry, she's so sorry, she should have listened. Abby asked the
medium if she could ask a question. 'I said I wanted to know
if it was on accident or if it was on purpose, and if it was on
purpose, do you take responsibility for putting yourself in that
situation?' She did not reveal what 'it' was. The medium said

'She's saying it wasn't an accident, and she's sorry for being there.'

If this tragedy had happened to one of her friends, Reeva would have been devastated. That's how she was, always caring for others. Family and friends meant the world to her. I want to channel her qualities into her legacy. Reeva believed love was all; that giving love and sharing love is such a positive emotion. Even when I got Bella, my puppy, eight months after Reeva died, she helped me so much to get through some dark months. I had to nurture her and she gave me so much love in return. From living a normal, quiet life I've had to come and live in the public eye, and I've had so much love from people. Wherever I go, people want to hug me. Reeva has inspired that love and that's a wonderful thing. It brings out the caring side in other people. As her mother, I loved her to the moon and around the world. We had the closest mother–daughter bond imaginable; we were the best of friends. But now I see Reeva Steenkamp has come to represent something much more resonant too.

Immediately after 14 February 2013, her name and image became the rallying point for campaigns against domestic abuse and gun violence. After the verdict, and Oscar Pistorius's culpable homicide conviction, her name became part of a debate about the South African judicial system – which again seems ironic for a law graduate whose ambition was to shine a spotlight on causes close to her heart. The law has deemed her fate to be the tragic result of someone else's recklessness and negligence. Some of the most senior attorneys in South Africa have expressed astonishment at the verdict. Oscar can't be tried again. He's had his trial and he's won. If he was a man in the street who didn't have money, he wouldn't have won in my opinion. The best legal team won. It cost him a lot of money, reported to be at least R100,000 per day. There had to be a winner and a loser, and we lost. Kristin, who studied law with Reeva, says she knew it would be difficult. The law is what it is. Our legal system is what it is. She was disappointed that we didn't get answers but her view is that the overwhelming public sentiment means he will live now in a permanent prison.

Sheena Jonker, who wrote that strong open letter to Oscar before the trial opened, gave her perspective on Facebook: 'What happened in Oscar's trial is how the system is designed to operate: the accused is presumed innocent until proven guilty, does not have to prove his innocence, but can test the state case to see if it is strong enough to prove guilt beyond a reasonable doubt, all the while simply advancing a version that may possibly fit with often compromised forensics. Compromised forensics in themselves are often enough to raise the requisite reasonable doubt, which is the only burden the defence has, to raise a reasonable doubt. So in this system if you can pay for

270

brilliant lawyers, this is often how things look. And within our legal framework, this is not unjust. But if one applies philosophies of natural justice, it is unjust. And it is not dissimilar all over the world and in other systems. The entire system operates on what facts can actually be established (proved) in court. And this often rails against the truth. South Africans beat themselves up wanting to see 'justice' in court. The truth is, a competitive adversarial system is just not the best platform for truth and justice. The truth may emerge, it may not. Sometimes it does. Sometimes it doesn't. And ultimately it is dependent on which side has the best lawyers and that is dependent on who can afford the best lawyers.'

People tell me the trial has also highlighted the problems inherent in broadcasting from criminal courts. It was a political decision to air it. Both sets of lawyers opposed televisation because it can inhibit witnesses and rouse extreme public feeling. Look at the OJ Simpson case in the United States and the Amanda Knox trial in Italy. It takes a long time to qualify, practise and understand law, but people watching snatches on TV become instant experts, confuse the issues and lambast the system. In the United Kingdom, Lord Chief Justice Lord Thomas said he had been 'very troubled' by what has happened in South Africa and proposed a 'pause' before going much further with televised proceedings in Crown Courts.

We'll leave those debates to the experts. As Barry says, we

just have to carry on with our normal lives. We're not the only ones in the world going through a crisis. We have to start life afresh. My way of dealing with the pain is to keep Reeva's spirit and ambitions alive. After the de-humanising affect of the court case, I want to reclaim Reeva as the caring, loving and moral human being she was and to re-assert the values she lived by. I'm not going to shrivel up and die. We plan to build a women's shelter in her name in Port Elizabeth. We're going to establish the Reeva Rebecca Steenkamp Foundation and raise money to build and run a shelter to give vulnerable women the skills and confidence to support themselves. That will be a fitting legacy. There is a need for support, security and protection beyond restraining orders. We want to provide not just a safe house, but a haven where women can learn how to be productive and support themselves independently. No one should have to tolerate ill treatment, but sometimes women do to keep a roof over their children's head. Education is key; the women can learn to bake, to knit, to study for a profession, to expand their horizons and regain their self-esteem.

Reeva was a gift, so precious. She was taken from us in her prime, not just at the height of her personal blossoming, but at a stage when she was poised to acquire a deeper role-model status in South African society. As Mrs Ntlangu said, our country has lost a role model: 'For us, as a country, to move forward, we need to communicate the races of this country and work together and Reeva was just that link. She loved people without barriers. For some people it's a new thing to work in this diverse world, but that child knew how to do it instinctively. She never saw colour in a person. She went out in the world and found it easy to work with people of all races, all backgrounds. The sad thing is that she could have changed the world.'

The past six months have been emotionally draining and physically wearing. I've had enough of sitting passively in court. I've always been a doer. I am busy planning a visit to an exemplary centre where I will learn how to set up and run a women's shelter on a professional and holistic model. It will be a multi-layered operation. It will be important to provide a support system with a network of doctors, nurses, centre mothers, attorneys, psychiatrists, teachers, all sorts of professionals, to enable these women to change their lives and regain their self-respect.

I'm sure this is what Reeva would have wanted as a legacy. She had taken the cause of vulnerable women and children to heart. To have her name emblazoned on an inspirational women's shelter will fulfil the 'professional ambassadorial' role she sought for herself as a young finalist in the Miss PE modelling competition while she is out there swimming with the dolphins, for ever young and spirited and free.

The Sentencing

On Tuesday 21 October 2014, Oscar Pistorius was sentenced to five years imprisonment for killing Reeva. Judge Thokozile Masipa also gave him a three-year suspended sentence for the firearms charge. The trial that had dominated our lives for nearly eight months ended with the sight of Oscar being taken down the stairs to the cells. He looked resigned. His family said they would not appeal; they had expected him to go to prison.

I felt so much better. Barry too. We feel justice has been done. We were happy with the sentence – five years is sufficient. Oscar will spend at least ten months incarcerated and it is right that he should pay for his actions. It was crucial to me that the sentence was also a message to society. I felt Judge Masipa gave a balanced consideration of the mitigating and aggravating arguments. She said 'a non-custodial sentence would send the wrong message to the community. On the other hand, a long sentence would also not be appropriate either, as it would lack the element of mercy.' She made the point that it would be a sad day for South Africa if there was a perception that it had one law for the rich and another for the poor.

We went to court hoping that the punishment handed down would fit the crime, and we left satisfied. It's been a long, long, harrowing journey and we are happy it is over. No sentence can ever provide absolute closure for us. Nothing can – unless someone can magic Reeva back. The man who took her life has to serve his time, but I don't want him to suffer. The Department of Correctional Services proved they will be able to cater for his special needs, and that was important to me. He will be well looked after.

After our disappointment with the verdict of culpable homicide, I said I was never going back to court. I changed my mind, however, because there had been talk of an appeal and of the judge having made a mistake with her summation, and I wanted to fill the courtroom with representations of how loved Reeva was. We wore her picture on our jackets, on water bottles, on notepads. Friends and family returned to Pretoria to hear the arguments in aggravation and mitigation of the sentence knowing it would be another ordeal during which Oscar's defence team would call witnesses to empha-sise everything he had lost, how much he was suffering, how vulnerable he was – and those arguments were always hard to sit through when our daughter, an innocent, lost her life and future and suffered a terrible death. Even the actual handing down of the sentence was like a seesaw – up, down, up, down – because the judge had to evaluate all the factors she had accepted or dismissed to explain how she reached the decision that was hers, and hers alone.

Some sort of closure came from Judge Masipa's acknowl-edgement of the damage wrought on our family. I was grateful for that. She said, 'Nothing I do or say can reverse what hap-pened to the deceased or her family,' – it was comforting to see she was now aware of our loss.

When Kim took the stand to speak on behalf of the family, the atmosphere was transformed at a crucial time. It was heartwrenchingly emotional. We were tremendously proud of Kim. She brought Reeva back to life as a person, giving her a voice in a room in which she had become invisible, just 'the deceased'. She did a fantastic job in reminding everyone why we were sitting in courtroom GD. Kim asked my per-mission to give her impact statement because she didn't want to upset me by talking so personally about Reeva and how heartbroken the family remains. She was nervous because she didn't want to let me down, and became intensely emotional herself, but she was strong, she pulled herself together, and I could see the judge listened intently to her every word. After Kim, Gerrie Nel did not need to put forward any further witnesses.

And so, we flew back to Port Elizabeth to start a new phase of life dedicated to raising money for the Reeva Rebecca Steenkamp Foundation which will set up shelters to help and empower other women. It will be a huge project to undertake in her memory, but one sustained by the love and support of so many people. Even as we left the High Court, offers of donations were coming in. As her mother, it is so comforting to see that Reeva continues to touch people. That was what my angel was all about – people and love.

Acknowledgements

My thanks go to:

Barry Steenkamp – my husband, my friend, my partner. The one who understands my pain and who supports me no matter what.

Jennifer and Hekkie Strydom – Jennifer has been my friend for many years, and I couldn't survive without her, EVER. She was like a mother to Reeva. She has been there for me through the good and the bad. Hekkie for emotional support to both Barry and myself and for allowing Jennifer to look after me throughout the trial.

Advocate Dup de Bruyn SC – for taking care of me throughout the trial. For his legal expertise, emotional support and friendship I will be forever grateful. He has been my protector and my doctor. Without him we would not be where we are today.

Truia de Bruyn – for invaluable emotional support and friend-ship. She was there in the beginning when Barry could not be.

Mike Venter (Attorney) – for his legal expertise and caring for us.

Tania Chanene Peace Koen (Attorney) – for legal advice, nev-erending support and her warmth. A wonderful and loveable person who I can depend on. And the neverending love and support of Taryn, Wesley and Tristan.

Sarah Thaw – for her hard work delving through mountains of e-mails, always with a smile.

ANC Woman's League – without whom I could not have been at the trial.

Jacqui Mofokeng – a stranger who has become a friend, and whom I believe could change the world.

Shoki Tshabalala – for supporting me even though she in times was in need of support.

Cindy and Clive Stoutjesdyk, Emily, Adam, Daniel and Nina – who supported me and made me feel like a new person through the pain.

Claire Myles – my friend of 30 years, who spent every weekend at my house and whose help on a daily basis I cannot do without.

Members of the public – whose messages of encouragement, love and support have been so wonderful and who come up to me to wish me well.

To all the Steenkamp family and all our friends for their love and support.

To Kristin Ellis, Abby Theron, the teachers at St Dominic's Priory School, Jane Celliers of ICE Models and Kim Martin for their reminiscences.

To Rebecca Winfield for her unwavering faith in the book and her hard work.

To Adam Strange, Rhiannon Smith and those at Little Brown for taking such care in putting together this book.

To Sarah Edworthy for putting my words and feelings on the page so eloquently and helping me to pay tribute to my beloved Reeva.